DISCOVERING SCIENTIFIC METHOD

Books by Hy Ruchlis

ORBIT

THE WONDER OF LIGHT

THE WONDER OF HEAT ENERGY

CLEAR THINKING

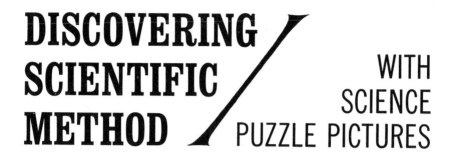

DISCOVERING SCIENTIFIC METHOD / WITH SCIENCE PUZZLE PICTURES

by Hy Ruchlis

Illustrated with Drawings by Jean Krulis
and with Photographs

HARPER & ROW, PUBLISHERS, NEW YORK, EVANSTON, AND LONDON

Contents

List of Puzzle Pictures

DISCOVERING SCIENTIFIC METHOD

I / The Nature of Scientific Method

Suppose that you were transported back in time to a small village in Europe some five-hundred years ago. America has not yet been discovered. The earth is still considered to be flat. The stars are believed to be little spots of light on a big dome that revolves around a fixed earth.

A peasant in this small village lives in a world that is much the same when he dies as when he was born. It is much the same a century before his birth as it will be a century after his death.

Suppose you try to explain to the peasant what the world of the twentieth century is like. "You sit in a chair at home and watch a screen that shows you what is happening a thousand miles away. On that screen you can also be shown things that happened a few hours ago or yesterday or ten years ago.

"You can get into a horseless carriage, turn a key, step on a pedal, shift a lever, and off it goes along a smooth, bumpless road at a speed twice as fast as the fastest horse can go.

"You climb up some steps into a big, cucumber-shaped house with wings on it. It speeds along the ground and zooms into the air. Soon you are five miles up. In less time than it takes to walk to town you can fly from Paris to Rome.

"A man steps into a tall metal tube, as high as a church steeple. There is a flash of flame from the bottom of the tube and a thundering roar. Then the tube rises into the air. In fifteen minutes that man is two-hundred miles up and zooming around the earth in an hour and a half, at a speed one-thousand times faster than a good horse can run. Millions of people on the ground are listening to him describe what he sees. Others on the ground are seeing just what he sees."

These events would surely seem miracles to the peasant—if he permitted himself to believe such fantastic nonsense. To some people whose lives have covered the span from the first automobile and radio to space flight and atomic energy, it must indeed seem to be a miracle. Hardly a week goes by without some new event that would have been considered earth-shaking at the turn of the century. After a while we get so used to change that it is taken for granted that scientists can do anything they wish, if only enough money is spent for research on the problem.

The peasant of olden times would probably not have believed that such vast changes were possible. Today some people have become so numbed by the rapid succession of startling events that they don't even blink an eyelash if they are told that the earth is five-billion years old, or that solid objects are really composed of tiny whirling particles of electricity with mostly empty space between them.

Along with a dramatic change in the physical environment of our world has come an equally drastic change in thinking and relations between people. The peasant would have been astounded at one of our election campaigns. Nobody ever heard of peasants getting together to elect their leaders. The lord of the manor told them what to do and they had to do it.

The peasant would have been equally astonished at one of our modern schools. As a child he had to go out into the field at eight years of age to help his father plow or the family would not have had enough to eat. To put almost all able-bodied boys and girls into school until the age of eighteen, and perhaps twenty-two or twenty-six, would have seemed utterly impossible. And how could so many people learn to do such difficult things as read, write, and calculate?

THE ROLE OF SCIENTIFIC METHOD IN CAUSING CHANGE

Many factors have operated to bring about these vast changes within the past two centuries. One of the most important has been the use of scientific method to obtain new knowledge about the world in which we live. This method is such a powerful tool for extracting the secrets of nature that the amount of knowledge is today doubling almost every decade. Millions of people are engaged in this pursuit of knowledge, where once there were only thousands, or perhaps hundreds. In fact it has been estimated that of all the scientists that ever lived, 90 percent are alive today.

This picture is quite spotty. While scientific method has been vigorously applied to prying secrets from atoms, it is far from being utilized in solving the much more important problem of stopping atomic destruction or of educating people to live in a changing world or of preventing over-population of the world. Many thoughtful people are becoming increasingly aware that it isn't enough to gather facts about "things." We must begin to apply scientific method to solving human problems as well as atomic problems.

Many doubt that scientific methods can be useful in this

area. They think of science as limited to objects and materials. You will hear a person say something like, "I don't like that artist. He is too scientific." Such a statement means that the artist is mechanical, perhaps measures everything with a ruler, and makes his circles with compasses. They associate science with humdrum calculations and not with such vital problems as electing a new president or solving social problems such as juvenile delinquency.

It is quite likely that we shall discover that scientific method goes beyond an ability to solve problems about "things," that it can be even more useful in solving problems between nations and in improving relations of individuals with one another. A recent report of President Kennedy's Science Advisory Committee urged greater scientific research into problems involving the affairs of people. The report enumerated some of the areas that could be tackled. These included: studies of family budgets, problems of businessmen and workers, movements of population, improving the use of leisure time, education of youth, preparation for careers, mental health, operation of the national economy, city and state planning, understanding of other peoples on earth.

We do not mean to imply that the only thing that counts in solving problems is scientific method. Among all peoples on earth, whether living in primitive or highly industrialized societies, there are fundamental similarities: friendship, family loyalty, and love—as well as enmity and hate. Generally speaking, humanity everywhere is characterized by friendly, cooperative relations among small groups of people, even if they hate people in another tribe or country. Scientific method doesn't directly determine whether people hate and kill, or love and cooperate. But if people see as a problem that there is too much hate and not enough love between different peoples, then they can call upon the established methods of scientific research to help them move in the direction in which they want to go. There is no reason why scientific method can't help us to understand ourselves better, just as it enables us to understand atoms better.

THE NATURE OF SCIENCE

We have talked about science and scientific method. But we haven't as yet said what they are. Like many other ideas in this world, such as those of beauty, justice, life, etc., it is difficult to provide simple, exact definitions that satisfy everybody. You will find a variety of definitions in books about science and no general agreement on any one. In the past, science was viewed as a body of knowledge based upon careful observation and logic and verified by means of experiment and additional observation. But many scientists are not completely happy with this kind of definition because it tends to narrow the role of science to a kind of grubby fact-gathering, limited to "things" and tedious note-taking. It doesn't adequately express the dramatic role or the tone of scientific method and the way in which it is beginning to be applied to many types of problems that were formerly considered outside the province of science.

A noted physicist, Percy W. Bridgman, has offered his version of a definition which is perhaps more suitable to recent developments in science: "Science means doing one's damnedest with one's brain, no holds barred."

The language is a bit strong—but it does convey the general feeling that scientific method involves the maximum use of our brains to *solve problems*. If the scientist, like the

5

artist, gets up suddenly in the middle of the night with an inspired thought that leads him to a new discovery, we shall simply consider it as part of the "no holds barred" approach. We may not be able to say how he does it, but that won't stop us from including it as an acceptable part of scientific method. However, there are many other aspects of the approach that we can describe in greater detail and which people can learn to use.

Let us first note that there is a weakness in the above definition if it is meant to include every possible activity of the human brain. We can imagine a bank robber using his brain "no holds barred," even to the extent of brilliantly planning a series of murders to gain his ends. During World War II some doctors in Nazi Germany used people as they would guinea pigs to discover the effects of chemicals or environmental changes on human beings. Science, as we know it today, is essentially humanist and seeks the betterment of humankind. We shall, therefore, adopt this feature as part of our definition. We shall change Dr. Bridgman's definition slightly to add this idea as well as to remove some of the strong language to which some people might object. After all, a definition should strive for universal acceptance. In such definitions we omit emotional words that may obstruct the meaning for some people.

"Science means using one's brain to solve problems for the betterment of humanity, no holds barred."

It should be noted that according to this broad definition it is possible for a businessman, a politician, an engineer, or a mechanic to be included in the category of "scientist." To the degree that people begin to incorporate scientific methods into their everyday life and work, to that degree will they become "scientists." Some scientists may not like this

6

broad definition and prefer to have an exclusive club to which only a few can be initiated. But most would agree that it is essential for humanity to begin to study the ways in which science has successfully solved extremely difficult problems and to apply them, insofar as possible, to *all* problems that mankind faces.

The best way to learn a procedure is to use it. A person who does not experience the method of science personally and who has not lived through the process of thinking scientifically will view it as some kind of mysterious "gadget" that someone else uses to pry open the secrets of nature. For that reason this book is devoted mainly to providing the reader with actual experience in using the method of science to pose and solve problems that will be raised by means of various photographs.

No miracles will be achieved by working out these problems. Before one can advance noticeably in the mastery of scientific method, he will require a great many more experiences—doing laboratory experiments at school and at home, adopting scientific attitudes in discussions of problems with friends and in the classroom, reading books that approach problems in a scientific manner, and living through many other similar experiences. If this book is but a start in that direction, it will have fulfilled its purpose.

WHAT IS SCIENTIFIC METHOD?

We might begin by saying that *scientific method is the basic set of procedures that scientists use for obtaining new knowledge about the universe in which we live.* We shall not include reading books or listening to a teacher describe facts as the really basic parts of the scientific method. These processes play a most important part in transmitting knowledge to others. But the books might state utter nonsense and the teacher could be quite wrong in his facts. If we rely fundamentally on such ways of gaining new knowledge, we can easily fall into the kind of situation wherein the "authorities" know best.

One of the main obstacles to development of new knowledge in the past has been the reverence in which the writings and teachings of some ancient philosophers were held. What they said often took precedence in any argument and tended to shut off further discussion or observation. Ancient men of learning (and some today) were afflicted by the "tyranny of certainty." It was the blind acceptance of what had been committed to writing that made it so difficult for fresh, inquiring minds to break through the barriers to new ideas.

Unless the teachings of the authorities in a subject are based upon scientific method, error can be just as easily transmitted as fact. Then people may emerge from the reading or hearing of the authorities' teachings quite certain of "facts" that are not so at all. Such mistrained people become a most serious obstacle to further advance in knowledge because they strenuously oppose the consideration of new ideas. In fact, it might reasonably be said that most of the history of science has been an account of how the misconceptions of previous generations had to be overcome by a few pioneers. If it weren't so difficult for people, including some scientists, to open their minds to new ideas, we would have advanced much further than we have.

The most important point to remember about the method of science is that it rests upon the attitude of the *open mind.* In accordance with this attitude one has the right to question *any* accepted fact. One who searches for truth has to learn to question deeply the things that are generally accepted as being "obviously true."

We must immediately warn against the "wise guy" who will seize upon this statement to justify having fun with his fellows by consciously questioning everything in a destructive manner. Many people love to hear themselves talk and need no better excuse than to be given the right to question everything. Sometimes it will be difficult to draw the line, and people who really want to know will be accused of destructive questioning. But that's a chance we will have to take. And the price for having to listen to several destructive questioners is the great value that the one real questioner can bring by discovering new truth.

IT IS EASIER TO BE WRONG THAN RIGHT

It may seem strange to suggest that there are no facts which can be proven positively, absolutely, and certainly beyond a shadow of a doubt. You may say, "I am certain that I exist." Yet, one could put up a good case for the idea that you are just a thought without physical reality. Perhaps you are just the programmed instructions in some giant other-world computer, and the things you think you observe are instructions as to what "you" should "see," "hear," or "feel." Who really knows?

Many "facts" believed in the past to be absolutely and certainly true have since been shown to be untrue. On the basis of this history one might even go so far as to say that *it is easier for men to be wrong than to be right.* After all, any brash child or ignorant adult can say anything he pleases about any subject under the sun. A learned man, who stops to think about the matter, may even be considered slow-witted and ignorant—by the ignorant. But most questions have more to them than is seen at a superficial glance. So the quick and easy answer—particularly to a new problem—is more likely to be wrong than right. Consider modern scientific answers to some ancient questions. Think of the attitude that a fifteenth-century man would take toward statements like these:

"When you look at an object, you see it because the lens in your eye forms an image on the back of the eyeball. This image is upside-down."

"When you touch something, you feel it because an electric current travels up to your brain. Then electrical signals may travel from your brain to different muscles, instructing them to move so as to grasp the object and perhaps lift it up."

"White light contains all the colors of the rainbow."

"Many common diseases are caused by tiny invisible plants and animals that get inside and feed upon us."

"There are small white objects in our blood (white blood cells) that move around through the spaces between parts of our bodies and eat up foreign creatures that happen to get inside."

"Most of the volume of what seems to be solid matter is really 99.99 percent empty space."

"Everybody and everything is made up mainly of electrical particles."

"The sun is so far away that it would take more than three-hundred years for the fastest horse to get there, if he could run without stopping, and if he had a road to follow. The sun is so big that a million earths could fit inside of its hot, glowing mass of gas. Internal temperatures range above a million degrees. *Everything* in it, including iron, is in the form of gas."

"There are billions of groups of stars (galaxies), each of which may contain billions of stars. They are so far away that it takes light two-million years to get to the nearest one, even though light can travel seven times around the earth in one second. Some of the farthest galaxies are so far away that it takes over a billion years for the light to reach us."

"When we look at the stars we see them as they looked many years ago. Some of the stars we see could disappear today and we wouldn't know it for perhaps a thousand years. They would still appear in the sky for all that time."

Each of these accepted facts would have seemed obviously false to most learned men of five-hundred years ago. On the basis of their "facts" they could well consider such statements serious evidence, if not proof, of lunacy.

The open mind is one important aspect of the *scientific attitude,* which lies at the base of the scientific method. A person who approaches a problem with a closed mind, unwilling to examine new facts, without any desire to make careful observations, and subject to the tyranny of certainty, has little or no chance of solving that problem properly. But a person with scientific attitudes, who knows how easy it is to be wrong, who examines new facts even if they seem to contradict his pet beliefs, who actually goes out hunting for such facts—such a person has a head start along the road to the solution of any problem he faces.

The development of scientific attitudes during the past five centuries and their adoption by increasing numbers of people probably have played an important part in the evolution of democratic forms of government. Our Founding Fathers lived at a time when science was beginning to flourish. An increasing number of people were seriously questioning the accepted beliefs of the time, not only in science but in such matters as "the divine right of kings." Many new ideas of that period were incorporated into the Constitution of the United States and the Bill of Rights. An important part in the development of these ideas was undoubtedly played by the previous two centuries of experience with scientific method in solving problems dealing with the earth, moon, sun, and planets.

The experience of the past indicates that improved functioning of democratic forms of government may depend in a major way upon the adoption by the general populace of scientific attitudes toward the solution of all problems, whether they be social, political and economic, or technological.

In general, then, scientific method may be viewed as a tool for solving all problems, no matter what their origin happens to be.

STATING THE PROBLEM

The application of scientific method starts with a problem of some kind. The problem can be anything one wishes to think about. It might be, "How far is the town of Inkling from the city of Outright?" Or it might be something more important, such as, "What is life?" Perhaps it is something personal like, "Should I study dentistry or engineering?" Then again, it might be, "How can we prevent people from losing jobs if a changeover from war industry to school and hospital construction is undertaken?"

It often happens that at a given time we just don't know enough to do more than speculate about a problem. This would have been true of a philosopher of three-thousand years ago who may have wondered about the moon. Were the gods really dragging it through the sky as he was told? What were the dark spots? Why did the moon change shape and repeat its changes about once a month? Such questions could not have been answered satisfactorily at that time because knowledge had not yet advanced to a point where it could be applied to this kind of problem. Nor had the instruments been developed to gather the kind of facts needed to solve the problem. But the fact that certain problems could not be solved at that ancient time did not mean they could *never* be solved. Similarly, there are many problems today to which it would seem there are no ways of finding solutions. But one never knows when a breakthrough in knowledge will occur to bring the problem within reach.

On the other hand there were problems that the ancient philosopher could have tackled if he had so desired. Seeing a strange insect on a rock, he might have taken the first step of wondering and posing questions. Where did it come from? Are there more like it around? How many legs does it have? How many wings? Does it help or harm man? Unlike those relating to the moon problem, these are questions of a kind that many ancient learned men could have asked and answered. Some did; most did not.

Like every other human endeavor, the ability to solve problems does not spring fullblown into a man's head. His way of thinking and his attitudes are molded by the times in which he happens to live. But basic changes in thinking do occur—generally rather slowly. Often such changes require generations or centuries of time although the pace of such change today is much faster than ever before. When we look back at ancient thinkers who helped change the times in which they lived, it is not fair to ask that they be superhuman, jump the centuries between us, and develop attitudes and ways of thinking which we have found so productive in recent times.

Each great civilization made its distinct contribution to the heritage of science and learning. Thus the ancient Egyptians and Babylonians made a great step forward when they began to think in terms of measurement, number, and simple mathematical shapes. They prepared the ground for the Greeks, who followed with an intensive development of mathematics. It is to them that we owe the development of the laws of logic, one of the main pillars of science.

Looking back at the work of ancient thinkers in the light of modern discoveries, we may perhaps see certain flaws in their work. They generally had a limited view of the place that man had in the universe. To them he seemed to be at the center of the stage, on a fixed earth, with all the heavenly bodies moving around it. They did not know that the universe is vastly more complex than they ever dreamed it could be. They had no idea how easy it is to be fooled by the senses and how much observation can be distorted by the expectations of the observer. The thinkers of that early time tended to feel that they could arrive at answers to problems mainly from within themselves, from their own thoughts. They did not feel the modern scientists' driving necessity for careful observation of nature to serve as the basis of thinking. Nor did they feel the need to test every thought by means of observation and experiment.

The big contribution of modern science to human thought is the understanding that creating new thoughts is but one part of the process of developing new knowledge. It is also necessary to laboriously gather facts as the food for such thought. And then, when the thoughts have been created, it is necessary to *test* them by devising experiments that will tell us if these thoughts conform to reality or not.

Scientists have learned how to be ruthless with ideas and speculations that do not meet the test of observation and experiment. They are thrown on the junk heap immediately. And if a speculation cannot be tested in some way, scientists waste little time arguing about whether or not it is true. They put it on the shelf until such time as the state of knowledge is advanced enough to enable them to test it again.

As an illustration of the modern approach to problems, consider the battle against cancer. Research in this field today revolves around a series of problems and sub-problems which are carefully spelled out by prolonged consideration of existing knowledge at conferences and in articles in scientific publications. Such problems are:

What factors in our environment increase or decrease the rate at which cancer develops?

Which chemical agents can cause cancer?

Which chemicals can slow down or stop the development of cancer?

May cancer be caused by viruses or other germlike organisms?

What conditions in our environment trigger cancer?

Does stress of any kind affect the onset or development of cancer?

Notice how each of these questions indicates a *direction for further experimentation or observation.* It takes a good scientist who already knows a great deal about the subject just to formulate questions like these and thereby map out a program of attack on the problem. The scientist of 1800 could not even have formulated some of these questions because some of them imply discoveries that were made later. For example, in 1800 we did not know of the existence of viruses. Thus the question about the effect of viruses could not even have been asked intelligently. Perhaps it might have been guessed at, but even so, the question would have been sheer speculation, like the ancient philosopher asking questions about the moon.

What kinds of judgments do scientists make when the facts are sparse? They generally limit themselves to formulating the problems properly and mapping out future lines of study rather than guessing in an area where nobody is competent to judge. As an illustration of this attitude, consider the following statement from an article "The Shelter-Centered Society" in *Scientific American* of May, 1962. This article summarizes the results of a discussion by a group of social scientists of the effects on the population of a program of building shelters.

"On one conclusion the conferees felt they could confidently agree: The existence of a shelter-centered civil defense would be a wholly new departure in U.S. history. Because the prospect is without precedent, they did not attempt to produce ironclad predictions of what would happen. They sought rather to define the problems that are likely to develop. As the product of their work together, the conferees issued not conclusions but a series of questions. They shared unanimously the sentiment that the questions are urgent and that action taken without careful consideration of these questions might lead to irreversible and disastrous consequences."

Most people adopt a less scientific approach to such matters.

GATHERING THE FACTS

Once a problem has been defined, the next stage is to gather information bearing on it. "No holds are barred" here. Books are examined, including ancient ones. Experiments are undertaken. Observations are made. All possible methods of obtaining information are used. Of course, how these methods are evaluated as to trustworthiness is an important part of the picture and involves its own complications, which we cannot penetrate too deeply in this brief account.

The organized gathering of facts about a problem was a giant step forward in the development of science. It began to occur on a large scale about four-hundred years ago.

This aspect of scientific method is the main difference between ancient and modern ways of obtaining knowledge. As we have noted, it isn't that there were no bright people in ancient days or that they never did any observing. Some were very observant. But by and large, learned men sat around and discussed problems based on their past experience, without really bothering to go out and dig up the facts the hard way. It was easier to *imagine* what would happen if you dropped a heavy object and a light one at the same time than to climb to the top of a tall building and drop them. Such practical procedures were often considered by the ancient Greek philosophers as equivalent to the everyday work performed by their slaves, and not at all suitable or fitting for philosophers.

Today when a great scientist proposes a new idea, other scientists don't just say, "It must be so because the great scientist Dr. X said it." Instead they ask, "What experiments can we devise that will provide evidence for or against this new idea?" Until they can gather facts that verify the new idea, they do not accept it as anything more than a proposal to be tested. In modern research it takes many related, supporting facts to prove that a new idea is true.

This illustrates another basic characteristic of scientific method. Ideas are never accepted as true just because someone says they are true. They must be *checked and verified by many competent observers* before being accepted into the body of knowledge.

BUILDING UP THE BODY OF KNOWLEDGE

Fact-gathering plays a basic role in the development of science. We make observations, thereby gathering facts. These facts lead us to wonder. As a result problems arise and questions are formulated. So we gather more facts. Where possible, we try to devise *experiments* that will produce a large number of facts. At a certain point we may have enough facts to develop some basic thinking about the problems.

Interwoven in this process is the use of a great deal of creative imagination to point the way to new directions for fact-gathering and for development of theories about the nature of underlying events. When confronted with a problem, we can imagine an infinite number of possible solutions. For example, when Newton asked, "What makes an apple fall?" he might have projected a wide variety of possible answers like these:

A witch living under every square foot of earth pulls all objects down.

Invisible strands pull the object back to earth.

Outer space pushes all objects together.

The earth is surrounded by an invisible stretchy coating,

like a balloon. When you lift anything, the coating is stretched and pulls the object back to earth.

There is a god whose job it is to see that all objects come back to earth.

You can imagine many more like these. Each of the suggested answers is an *hypothesis*, a guess at a possible solution to the problem.

Anyone can invent different hypotheses. But it takes a genius like Newton to cut through the vast number of possible hypotheses to pick out the ones that are likely to be fruitful under further investigation.

Of course a good *working hypothesis* doesn't exist in a vacuum. It must be based on previous knowledge. Thus, on the basis of what scientists had learned about nature before Newton's time, he would not waste time making up hypotheses about the falling apple that included ideas about witches and gods. On the other hand, it had already been shown that the earth and planets revolved about the sun and that the moon revolved about the earth. It was therefore reasonable for Newton to try to connect the falling of the apple and the revolution of the moon about the earth by imagining that both motions were caused by the same kind of force—gravity.

Notice that this hypothesis would not have made much sense if people believed that the moon was pulled through the sky by a horse and chariot driven by a god.

An hypothesis merely provides a direction for further investigation. If an hypothesis is not pursued, it has no more merit than any other hypothesis that can be made about a problem. But if the process is scientific, facts must be gathered to test the truth or falsity of the hypothesis. In Newton's case he spent some twenty years trying to show by means of calculation that his hypothesis could explain the observations about the motions of the moon and planets.

Actually, in a complex situation there are usually several hypotheses rather than one. They may come at different times in the course of trying out various solutions to a problem.

As we work with an hypothesis or group of hypotheses and test them in various ways, we begin to get some idea as to whether or not they conform to reality. We may reach a stage at which the hypothesis (or group of hypotheses) has a substantial amount of evidence in its favor, although we are not yet certain that it is correct. At that point we begin to consider the set of hypotheses to be a *theory*. But the search for new evidence continues in the same way. Each new fact that supports the theory continues to strengthen it. Each correct prediction made from the theory helps to solidify it.

One of the strongest kinds of evidence for an hypothesis or for a theory is its accuracy when it is used to predict events. Our creative imagination leads us to think of different situations in which the hypothesis or theory can be applied. We predict what will happen on the basis of the hypothesis or theory. Then we devise an experiment or look for a situation in which we can test the prediction. For example, Newton proposed the hypothesis that the force of gravity should become less as one goes up from the surface of the earth. He also predicted the exact degree of reduction with increasing height. Subsequently the reduction of the force of gravity with height was measured by means of accurate instruments and found to be what Newton predicted.

Eventually, if all the evidence supports a theory and none contradicts its basic ideas, the theory may come to be accepted as fact. We may then refer to such an accepted theory as a *principle* or a *law*. Thus we now refer to the "Law of Gravitation" and to "Newton's Laws of Motion" because there is such a vast accumulation of evidence that supports them.

Of course we must always maintain an open mind about any such laws and principles, no matter how certain we may be about them. Some new experiment or observation may cast doubt on what we consider to be laws. We must examine such facts most carefully because they often lead to new insights into familiar events and open up new lines of investigation.

This actually happened at the turn of the century. An experiment performed by Michelson and Morley could not be explained adequately by applying Newton's ideas about motion and gravitation. Einstein made a new set of hypotheses which modified them. These hypotheses were developed by him into the theory of relativity, which is still being tested today in various ways. Although the evidence supporting Einstein's theory is strong, it is by no means final and may never be. New facts may be uncovered that require us to question the theory of relativity or to modify it, as was done with Newton's theories.

Gradually, out of this kind of process, an interlocking structure of fact is created. This becomes the basis upon which the next generation of scientists continue their work. Slowly the structure builds up and our body of knowledge grows.

Today, as a result of this process, we have accumulated so much knowledge that it is no longer possible, as it once was, for men to do more than master one tiny segment of what is known.

The process of recording information in books and passing it on to young people in our schools plays a vital role in building knowledge. One important reason why modern science can advance so rapidly is that it isn't necessary for a scientist to work from scratch every time he starts on a problem. He can get an immense head start by reading about it in books and scientific journals. A great deal of attention, therefore, is paid to the accuracy of such books and articles. Errors very often creep in. But if anyone discovers an error, he will generally so inform the author and the publisher. Then corrections are published for other readers to note.

One of the toughest of the problems faced by scientists today is just keeping up with the mountain of new information as it comes out. Experiments now under way with giant computers may make it possible for these machines to store information and quickly produce it in a form suitable for a particular problem.

THE ROLE OF INSTRUMENTS AND MEASUREMENT

The fact-gathering process itself is given a great deal of attention by scientists. As we shall see in later sections of this book, it is quite easy for our senses to be fooled. Magicians do it every day of the week. Most of the time we don't even realize that we are being misled by our senses because we rarely have occasion to check the "facts" our senses gather. As an illustration, consider the lines AB and BC in Fig. 1. Which is longer? Or are they the same length? First make your judgment. Then measure with a ruler. What do you find?

FIG. 1

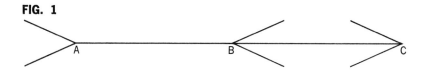

This "experiment" indicates why scientists prefer to gather facts by means of instruments that aid their senses. Each instrument is better adapted to help gather facts of a given type than the unaided senses. A ruler is better at measuring lengths—provided that you use your eyes properly in handling the measurements. A clock provides more accurate comparison of intervals of time. A microscope is essential for viewing small objects; a telescope for distant objects. An enormous variety of complex instruments has been developed to ferret out different kinds of facts. We have spectroscopes to study stars, atoms, and chemicals. Magnetometers and vibration recorders are used to detect the presence of underground oil. Seismographs are needed for detecting earthquakes and perhaps distant atomic explosions.

Instruments are used to obtain observations of a kind that we could not obtain with our unaided senses. We generally attempt to assign number values to our observations. Such a number-valued observation is called a *measurement*. The measurement enables us to describe the fact in much more useful detail.

For example, an astronomer wishes to describe the sun and the moon. He can say, "The sun is much, much, much bigger than the moon." Or he can say, "The diameter of the sun is about 860,000 miles. The diameter of the moon is about 2,000 miles. The ratio of diameters is about 430 to 1. It would require about 80 million moons to fill up a globe the size of the sun." You can see that the comparison of sizes using numbers based upon measurement provides much more information and understanding than the statement "much, much, much bigger."

A number of problems in this book will provide practice in using measurements to gather facts. Our instruments will be simple: ruler, protractor, compass. But even with these simple instruments we shall be able to gather enough important facts to make interesting discoveries.

THE ROLE OF REASONING

With the passage of time, science comes more and more to rely upon the tool of mathematics to dig far deeper into the unknown than our ordinary experience can take us.

Newton's ideas about gravitation and orbits and Einstein's Theory of Relativity were derived largely through the use of mathematical reasoning. These new ideas gave man the power to go beyond what he experiences and to extend knowledge to the vast reaches of outer space.

The use of mathematics is part of the process of reasoning which we employ as a basic tool of scientific method. One might say that the status of a body of knowledge as a science depends upon the degree to which mathematical methods are applied to it. Many social scientists are striving to raise the level of their knowledge by applying mathematical techniques to the solution of their problems.

There are two basic ways of using reasoning to obtain new information. One is the *inductive* method. The other method is known as *deductive*.

Here is an example of reasoning by induction:

Suppose that you are seeing a piece of paper burning for the first time. Your observations might be stated something like this:

Observation 1: That piece of paper thrown into the fire burned up.

Observation 2: This second piece of paper thrown into the fire also burned up.

Hypothesis, stated as a problem: I wonder if all paper burns?

Experiment: Let's try throwing many different kinds of paper into the fire. Here are ten more pieces to test.

Observation 3: Paper A burned.

Observation 4: Paper B burned.

And so on, until all ten pieces of paper have been thrown into the fire and have been observed to burn.

If we wished to state the results of this experiment, it would be a waste of time to enumerate the specific facts about all twelve pieces of paper. We can summarize the information with a statement such as, "All twelve papers burned up when put into the fire." This statement is a *conclusion* that summarizes our observations.

Now, on the basis of this experience with twelve pieces of paper, we may wish to extend our conclusion beyond the limits of the experiment, or *extrapolate,* by assuming that the same thing will hold true for *all* papers, not just the twelve we happened to try to burn. We *generalize* the statement and say, "All paper burns when thrown into a fire." We may drop the word "all" and say, "Paper burns when thrown into a fire," but the idea that the statement applies to "all" still remains.

You will observe that although the *generalization* summarizes our experience, it also projects beyond it to cover events of the same kind elsewhere and in the future. It therefore has somewhat the same nature as an hypothesis, which points the way toward further testing. But the generalization is more than a simple hypothesis in that it is based upon a substantial amount of fact. It helps us summarize experience and bring order out of chaos. We use it to classify and organize our observations into compact statements which provide guides to future events. For example, in the case of our statement about papers burning we can predict from the generalization that any particular paper that we may happen to pick up any place on earth, at any time, will probably burn up if put into a fire.

If we try burning different kinds of paper in different places and at different times and we find that they always burn up, then we soon come to consider the generalization as an established fact.

Of course one would never be absolutely sure that the generalization is really true for all kinds of paper in all places and at all times. One would never know whether *all* paper burns in a fire until every last piece of paper in the world and all past, present, and future pieces of paper had been burned up. Obviously we have to be practical. We can't base our generalizations on too few observations, and we can't afford the time and effort of making too many. It is a matter of judgment as to how many observations should be made to be reasonably sure of a generalization. In real life it often happens that even the experts make serious errors in assessing the number of observations they need to be sure of some fact.

As an illustration consider the problem faced by medical scientists in evaluating the safety of drugs. If a drug has been tested and found safe in ten-thousand applications over a period of five years, how can one be sure that damaging effects will not show up after another ten years of use? How can one be sure that the drug may not have dangerous effects under certain special conditions such as childbirth, different climate, or in combination with other drugs?

For example, thalidomide, a drug used to induce sleep, was recently marketed after being found "safe." The observations regarding its safety were made during several years of experimentation. Since it was an effective sleeping pill and also had the special advantage of being safe even when taken in large doses, it came into widespread use in Europe. But it was kept off the market in the United States because a doctor in the Department of Health was not quite sure that enough observations had been made.

Then doctors in Europe began to notice an increasing number of cases in which babies were born with deformed limbs. Sometimes limbs were completely missing. They began to trace the case histories of the mothers who had had such babies. Most were found to have taken these sleeping pills prior to the birth of their babies. With further investigation it was established that the sleeping pills were definitely the cause of the deformed or missing limbs.

In this case, failure to obtain enough observations led to a faulty generalization that the drug was safe and caused tragedy in many thousands of families.

The term *conclusion* indicates an end to a specific reasoning process. In that sense every generalization from observations is a conclusion. But there is a serious danger to scientific reasoning in the way many people use the word conclusion. They give it a kind of finality which it really does not have in scientific discovery. One may end up with a conclusion, take a breather, and then go to work extending it into new areas by asking additional questions about it and devising new experiments to bring forth new observations.

At any rate you can see the general nature of the inductive process. We gather many observations about a problem, often as the result of experiments designed for the purpose. If possible, we attempt to summarize the observations with a *generalization*. Acceptance as a fact will come after many others have checked the generalization many times and found it to be a correct statement.

In contrast to the inductive process we often develop new information on the basis of making *deductions*. Consider the following two statements:

1. An insect is an animal with 2 wings, 6 legs, and antennae.

2. Here is a new animal that has 8 legs, no wings or antennae.

From these statements it *necessarily follows* that:

3. The strange animal is not an insect.

Statement number three is a *deduction* from the other two statements, called the *premises*. It is also a conclusion, an end to this particular reasoning process. But unlike the generalization made by induction, the deduction is a *necessary consequence* that follows automatically from the premises. Unlike a statement made as a result of the inductive process, we are sure of the deduction, provided that the statements upon which it is based are *accepted as true*. Any question about the truth or falsity of the conclusion must be referred to the truth or falsity of the premises.

Regardless of whether or not the two premises are true or false, the deduction from those premises is *valid* because it is correctly made. Yet such a valid deduction may be a false statement about real things in the world.

When we come to science, however, we are very much concerned with whether or not a deduction is really true to life. So the scientist goes about checking all premises and deductions just as thoroughly as he does the generalizations made by induction.

In any real situation the reasoning process always involves a back and forth interplay between induction and deduction. We gather facts and make generalizations inductively. Then we operate with these generalizations to make deductions. Thereafter we check the truth of both deductions and generalizations against reality by means of more experiments and fact-gathering. And so our knowledge grows.

SCIENCE PUZZLE PICTURES

There is much more that can be said about scientific method, but we have indicated enough of its main features to serve as a guide. The remainder of the book is devoted to specific problem-solving experiences involving Puzzle Picture photographs. These provide varied experiences from which a variety of lessons about scientific method may be learned.

In order to obtain full value from these experiences it is important that you participate as fully as you can in posing questions and solving the problems. To provide practice in formulating questions based on your own observations, each Puzzle Picture problem starts with a photograph. In a few cases attention may be directed to specific features which will be the subject of discussion, but in most cases you will be completely on your own in determining the direction your questions are to take.

Be sure to spend some time observing the photographs carefully and asking questions about them. The questions posed in the book may or may not be the same as yours. It really doesn't matter. It's the practice that counts. Of course you will be pleased if you propose the same questions. In some cases you will be surprised at how much you did not observe. And then there will be the thrill of posing your own questions and perhaps answering them from clues in the photographs.

After you have posed some questions, turn the page and read the questions in the book. But don't go any further yet! Don't look at the discussions that follow the questions until you have really made an attempt to answer them yourself. You will lose much of the value of this practice in using scientific method if you jump right to the answers to the questions. You will also get more fun out of the problems if you try to arrive at some of the answers by yourself.

Of course if you have really tried and can't answer all the questions, then, after a reasonable time, read the analysis of the Puzzle Picture. In that section you will see how one goes about solving problems by means of the interplay of observation, induction, deduction, previous knowledge, common sense, and any other mental processes that can help.

As we have seen, the method of science has been defined as using one's brain to solve problems, "no holds barred." Anything goes, so long as it is honest and not a trick. If you happen to know a particular fact from your experience, you can use it to help solve any one of the problems posed. Many of the problems involve facts of this nature. In some Puzzle Picture problems you may be asked to make measurements with a ruler and perhaps to make scale drawings. Such procedures will provide valuable experience in using measurement and calculation in real situations.

The Puzzle Pictures have been grouped under a number

of headings, such as *General Principles, Observations, Scientific Reasoning,* and *Measurement and Mathematics.* These groupings are not meant to be taken in a narrow sense. Actually, many aspects of scientific method apply to each Puzzle Picture, and our classification is purely for convenience in organizing the basic ideas.

With this brief introduction let us proceed to consider the nature of scientific method in greater detail by studying specific situations presented in our science Puzzle Pictures.

II / General Principles

The Puzzle Picture problems in this chapter are designed to bring out certain basic principles of scientific method, some of which have already been touched upon in a general way in the previous chapter.

Although all Puzzle Pictures in the book involve various degrees of observation, formulation of questions, use of inductive and deductive reasoning, making and checking hypotheses, those in this chapter involve questions that feature a specific important lesson, as you shall soon see.

PUZZLE PICTURE A. DRIVER'S DILEMMA?

The driver of this car seems strangely unconcerned with the plight of the poor fellow on the ground. His attitude should raise some interesting questions in your mind.

DRIVER'S DILEMMA?

The nonchalant attitude of the driver in Puzzle Picture A makes it clear that there is really nothing to worry about. The strong man on the ground has been practicing this trick for some time and is simply putting on a display for the photographers.

But this event does provide us with some questions:

1. Why isn't the man on the ground injured?
2. How did the car get into that position?
3. When was this picture taken?
4. Where was it taken?

Analysis of Puzzle Picture A

(*Remember: Don't look at the answers until you have tried to answer the questions yourself.*) The photograph illustrates the fact that we have to "expect the unexpected" and be prepared to modify our body of "facts" in the light of new experience. Before looking at this picture you would probably have accepted it as a fact that a person who found himself under the wheel of a car would certainly be injured. But here you see that this is not always so. With proper training one can withstand the unusual forces involved.

However, a new aspect of scientific work interests us in this case. When you see an unusual event of this kind, it is natural to try to explain how it could happen. But wondering about it and actually explaining it are quite different activities. Let us see how a scientist would go about explaining the unusual event pictured in this photograph.

1. The weight of a car is supported by four wheels, with approximately one fourth on each wheel. The old-fashioned kind of car shown in the photograph probably

weighed about 3,000 pounds. So the weight on the man was
$\frac{1}{4} \times 3,000$, or about 750 pounds.

The total amount of force is not the only thing that deter-
mines the effect upon the man on the ground. A great deal
depends upon how that force is distributed over the area of
his body. This distribution of force over an area is ex-
pressed in the idea of *pressure*. For example, if 10 pounds
rest on 2 square inches, the pressure is $\frac{10 \text{ lbs.}}{2 \text{ sq. in.}}$, or 5 lbs. per
square inch (abbreviated *psi*).

If the same 10 lbs. rest on $\frac{1}{2}$ sq. in., then the pressure is
$\frac{10 \text{ lbs.}}{\frac{1}{2} \text{ sq. in.}}$, or $10 \times \frac{2}{1}$, or 20 psi. It isn't that there are 20 lbs.
of force. There are never more than 10. But the *concen-
tration* of the 10 lbs. on $\frac{1}{2}$ sq. in. is, in effect, the same as
produced by 20 lbs. on 1 sq. in.

If the 10-lb. weight rests on the point of a thumbtack
that has an area of only $\frac{1}{10,000}$ sq. in., then the pressure is
10 lbs. on $\frac{1}{10,000}$ sq. in., or $10 \times \frac{10,000}{1}$, or 100,000 psi.
This enormous pressure is what punctures a wooden sur-
face when you press with a rather small force on a thumbtack.

Note that pressure can be high for two reasons: 1) the
force is large, and 2) the area is small.

The air pressure in the tires of a car may be only 25 psi,
yet it can easily hold up the weight of the car. We simply
need enough square inches for the pressure to act. If the
car weighs 3,000 lbs., then $\frac{3,000}{25}$, or 120 sq. in., would be
enough to support the weight. Check this calculation by

35

noting that 25 lbs. per sq. in. on each of 120 sq. in. could support 25 × 120, or 3,000 lbs.

Assuming that each tire must support one fourth of the car's weight of 3,000 lbs., an area of ¼ of 120 or 30 sq. in. would suffice to accomplish that task. This area is equivalent to that of a rectangle 3 in. wide by 10 in. long.

If a car is raised off the ground and then slowly lowered, you see the tires gradually flatten out against the ground. As the tires get flatter the area of contact increases. Soon the total area is 120 sq. in., and the weight of the car can be supported completely by the air pressure. The car does not sink any lower (unless weight is added).

If the tires lose air, the pressure in the tires drops. Then the tires flatten a bit more until there are enough additional square inches to make up for the loss of pressure and still hold up the weight.

Now let's apply these facts to our friend under the car.

The tire resting on the man's abdomen is relatively smooth with no sharp points. So, the weight is distributed rather evenly. And as the tire sinks into his soft body the surface of contact probably increases to more than the 30 in. normally required on hard ground. Perhaps there are 50 sq. in. of contact. In that case the 750 lbs. of weight on one tire, supported by 50 sq. in., exert a pressure on him of $\dfrac{750 \text{ lbs.}}{50 \text{ sq. in.}}$, or 15 lbs. per square inch. This is the same as the normal pressure of the atmosphere on our bodies. But of course this pressure from the weight of the tire is in addition to the normal air pressure already acting on the man.

Of course the effects of the distributed weight of the car

and that of the air are not quite the same because air pressure is exerted perfectly evenly all around our bodies and also inside our lungs—pressing outward. The pressure caused by the weight of the car is only on the abdomen. But at least you can see that it is not unreasonable to expect a very strong man to be able to support such a pressure.

2. Another important reason why the man is not injured is that the pressure on him was increased rather gradually and not too suddenly. Although the picture does not show us what happened before it was snapped, it would seem likely that the car was not simply run over his body. If it were, as the wheel hit one side of his body the areas of contact would be small and pressures would be quite high. His muscles would not be in the proper places to support the pressures. And he would be unprepared for them.

One way to get the car wheel on his body more gradually is to drive the car slowly up a small ramp placed at his side. The car can be backed down along such a ramp to release him. Or a jack can be used to lift the car and then lower it onto his body. Then the jack can be removed while the picture is taken. Later the jack can be put back to lift the car and release him.

3. The license plate reads "1945." It is not likely that old license plates would be put on a car, so we may infer that the picture was taken in 1945.

4. The Illinois license plate indicates that it is highly probable (but not certain) that the picture was taken in Illinois.

There are several lessons about scientific method that can be learned from this discussion:

1. Events that, at first glance, seem to be improbable may be reasonably explained by careful analysis of the situation.

2. Mathematical reasoning can be very helpful in such an analysis.

3. Knowledge of fundamental principles of science plays an important part in such reasoning.

PUZZLE PICTURE B.   AN INTERESTING VIEW

This photograph of a car on a flooded city street should suggest some interesting questions. But don't rush your observations or you will miss some important details in this picture.

(WIDE WORLD PHO

AN INTERESTING VIEW

A strange feature of Puzzle Picture B is that you can see the underside of the car. Are you below the level of the car? It would seem so, otherwise how could you see the underside?

And why is the car standing on another one that is upside down? Is this a trick photo? Or is it a mirror reflection in quiet water in a street? But, since you can see the underside of the car, doesn't it follow that the photographer must have been below the level of the car? And then wouldn't the water be running downhill toward the photographer? If it were moving downhill, would it be quiet enough to give a mirrorlike reflection?

It seems all mixed up. But don't throw up your hands in despair. You can solve the mystery if you try. Give yourself a chance to do so. Then read the analysis that follows.

Analysis of Puzzle Picture B

This photograph is an optical illusion created by viewing the original picture upside down. View the picture in its correct position by inverting the book. The picture now seems perfectly normal. It is a simple scene on a side street in some town or city, with a pool of still water giving an almost perfect reflection.

Note that when you see the photograph in its correct position, you cannot see the underside of the car, but it does appear in the reflection. When the picture is inverted, the image of the reflection is on top and shows a view of the underside of the car. This reversal causes the strange appearance of the car when the picture is viewed upside down. Other parts of the upside-down picture also seem

PUZZLE PICTURE C.   THE PROBABILITY OF EVENTS

This seems to be just an ordinary harness race. But something

strange because you get a different view in a reflection than in a direct view.

The reflected image is almost perfect because there is little wind or other disturbance and the water is extremely flat. Note, however, that the reflection is dimmer than the original scene. Also, small ripples in some parts of the pool create slight distortions. You can find such distortions in several regions of the reflection.

Look at the picture again, as you first viewed it. Note the strange appearance of the hydrant, of the nearest tree, and of the houses. All seem to be sticking up through the ground in a most peculiar manner. Actually they appear as

unusual happened here. See if you can discover what was so different about this event. Then try to formulate a question about it.

though viewed from below ground level over a slight rise (the rise of the sidewalk as compared with the street).

This photograph illustrates the scientific principle that flat, smooth surfaces reflect light in such a way as to provide mirror images of the same size and shape as the original objects, but from a different viewpoint.

The important thing we can learn from our analysis of this picture is that *appearances can be deceiving if a situation is altered in some way to which we are not accustomed.* Unless we are prepared to meet such situations with an open mind, we can easily draw incorrect conclusions as we attempt to relate what we observe to what is familiar.

THE PROBABILITY OF EVENTS

There are no absolutely certain facts in real life. No matter how much *evidence* we find to *prove* a certain fact, there is always the chance that deeper study will reveal new evidence that could cause us to modify our statement of the fact.

We express the strength of the evidence for a statement and the extent to which it is considered to be "proved" by referring to the *probability* that the statement is true. In mathematics a probability of 1 means that an event is certain. A probability of 0 means that it never happens. With regard to a statement about an event, a probability of 1 might be taken to mean that we are certain it is true. A probability of 0 would be taken to mean that the statement is false. A probability of ½ would be taken to mean that we consider it equally likely to be true or false.

In most situations it is not possible for us to calculate the exact degree of probability. It is necessary to rely to a large extent on judgment, and there will be considerable variation in such judgments. In such cases we express our judgments by using expressions like these:

almost certain
very likely (highly probable)
likely (probable)
fifty-fifty chance (equal probability of occurrence and non-occurrence)
unlikely (low probability)
very unlikely (very low probability)
almost never (probability almost zero)

There are times when it is possible for us to assign a numerical value to the probability of an event. For example, suppose one were to make this statement about the outcome of a horse race: The horses in a race cross the finish line in a consecutively numbered order.

Most of us would realize that this is not a likely event for a group of horses in a race since we can imagine them crossing the finish line in a great variety of different numerical orders. In fact, our experience might lead us to think that it "couldn't happen" if the group were quite large. In any case, such an occurrence would be quite unlikely.

Yet Puzzle Picture C shows that it actually *did* happen for this group of seven horses. They crossed the finish line in the order of their numbers: 1, 2, 3, 4, 5, 6, 7.

Now answer these questions:

1. What is the chance that this event will occur?
2. If 10,000 horse races take place each year throughout the world, how often would we expect to see such an event?

Analysis of Puzzle Picture C

1. Let us restrict the calculation to a race among seven horses.

The chance that horse number 1 will come in first in a group of seven is $\frac{1}{7}$. In other words we would expect this event to happen about once every seven times. The event is not likely, but we certainly wouldn't rate it as "very unlikely." In 10,000 races we would expect it to happen $\frac{1}{7} \times$ 10,000 times, or 1,428 times.

If horse number 1 comes in first, this leaves six horses to fight it out for second place. Now the chance that horse number 2 will come in ahead of the others is one out of six times, or $\frac{1}{6}$. The chance that both events will happen in the

43

same race—that is, horse number 1 coming in first and horse number 2 coming in second—is seen to be $\frac{1}{6}$ of $\frac{1}{7}$, or $\frac{1}{42}$.

By applying similar reasoning to all seven horses we see that the chance that the horses will finish in the order 1, 2, 3, 4, 5, 6, 7 is: $\frac{1}{7} \times \frac{1}{6} \times \frac{1}{5} \times \frac{1}{4} \times \frac{1}{3} \times \frac{1}{2} \times 1$. This amounts to $\frac{1}{5,040}$. In other words, in a large number of races we would reasonably expect this event to occur about once in 5,000 times, on the average.

2. If there are 10,000 races a year all over the world, and if the horses are numbered in consecutive order (assuming 1 to 7), then we would expect the event to happen $\frac{1}{5,000} \times 10,000$, or about two times a year.

Of course our guess of 10,000 races a year is very rough, at best. But you can see that for this number of races we would expect the event to happen a few times each year. Thus, although we would rate the event as very unlikely, we wouldn't consider it in the "almost never" class.

Actually, you can see that there may be some difference of opinion as to exactly what is meant by "almost never." For that reason scientists prefer, if possible, to state their probabilities as numbers like $\frac{1}{5,040}$, rather than in general terms.

PUZZLE PICTURE D.   NOON SHADOW

This simple street scene was snapped in a town in southern
Mexico at latitude 16° N. on July 1 at noon. What questions might
you ask about this scene, particularly about the shadow of the pole?

NOON SHADOW

In Puzzle Picture D there is a clear shadow of the pole on the ground. Can you figure out which way is north, using the shadow as your guide?

Analysis of Puzzle Picture D

You are familiar with the fact that the sun is south of us at noon and therefore casts shadows toward the north at that time. Thus the noon shadow of a pole should point north.

We observe in the photograph that the shadow of the pole is to the right. We have been informed that the picture was taken at noon. It would then seem to be an obvious deduction that north is to the right.

However, it is very important that we understand the limits of the "facts" we think we know. What is true under one set of conditions may not be true under another set of conditions. For example, is it a fact that summer begins on June 21? Yes, if one is referring to the Northern Hemisphere. No, if one refers to the Southern Hemisphere. A complete statement of the facts about summer and winter requires a definition of the words "summer" and "winter," plus reference to the different seasons north and south of the equator.

It is a fact that a noon shadow points north in all parts of the United States at all times of the year. But in Buenos Aires, Argentina, a noon shadow always points south. The reason for this is shown in Fig. 2.

Why do we select the United States and Buenos Aires for our examples? These places are in the Temperate Zone. Had we selected any place in the Torrid Zone, then we would find that the sun at noon is sometimes in the north-

FIG. 2

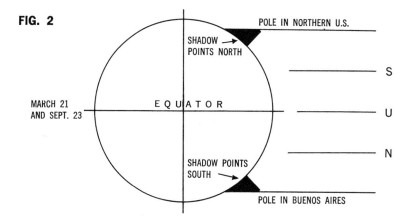

ern part of the sky and at other times in the southern part. As a result, noon shadows point north or south, depending upon the time of year.

On July 1 the earth is very close to the June 21 position for summer in the Northern Hemisphere. On June 21 the northern end of the earth's axis is tilted $23\frac{1}{2}°$ toward the sun. As a result, the sun is exactly overhead at latitude $23\frac{1}{2}°$, the Tropic of Cancer. Although the photograph was taken in Mexico at a latitude $16°$ north of the equator, the location of this region of the earth happens to be south of the place where the sun is overhead. This situation is shown in Fig. 3.

FIG. 3

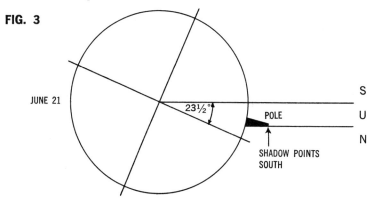

A slight change occurs by July 1, but it is not enough to alter our reasoning. The sun changes position very slightly in the week or so after June 21. Thus the situation on July 1 is essentially the same as on June 21.

From this reasoning we can see that the shadow of the pole points south in the photograph, not north. North is therefore to the left of the picture.

Remember the lesson here: *Facts are true only under specific conditions.* If the conditions are altered in important respects, one must expect changes to be required in the statement of the facts.

Consider the statement "Whatever goes up must come down." This would certainly have been accepted as a fact in the distant past. Recently, with the launching of earth satellites, conditions have changed. Today people would not accept this statement as completely true. It would have to be modified somewhat like this: "Whatever goes up must come down, unless it is going so fast in the proper direction that it orbits the earth or escapes from the earth's gravitational field."

Actually, you can see that the exception makes the original statement false. It is no longer true that "whatever goes up must come down."

As another illustration, consider how a resident of a warm South Sea island might view the nature of the water around him. He would certainly think that the following statement is true: "You can never walk on water because it is always liquid and would give way under your weight."

Under the conditions with which he is familiar, water *always* has this property. But all we have to do is lower the temperature to 32° F. and liquid water changes to solid ice. Then he can walk on it with ease. If our South Sea

48

islander has never seen this happen, he has good reason seriously to doubt your sanity if you try to convince him that under certain conditions his experience with water would no longer apply.

Scientists view their facts as "true" for the conditions under which observations are made. They may speculate that the truth will apply under different conditions, but they will never really know until they actually have experience with these new conditions.

PUZZLE PICTURE E.   AN UNUSUAL MOON PICTURE

You are familiar with the many craters that cover much of the moon's surface. But in this photograph of a portion of the moon we observe plateaus and mounds. What questions might you ask about this picture?

(PHOTOGRAPH FROM THE MOUNT WILSON AND PALOMAR OBSERVATORIES)

AN UNUSUAL MOON PICTURE

There are many questions you could ask about Puzzle Picture E. In Puzzle Picture F we shall refer to this photograph in greater detail, but right now we wish to pose just one question to illustrate some interesting points about scientific method: Why does this region have so few craters and so many raised portions of land?

Analysis of Puzzle Picture E

(Make a real effort to answer the questions by yourself before you read the analysis that follows.)

The mounds and hills are really craters, but their misleading appearance is the result of an optical illusion. Invert the book and view the picture "upside down." Now you can see concave craters. Rotate the book and view the photograph from different angles. Note how the appearance of the craters changes when the picture is upside down.

You probably have not seen this particular illusion before because printed pictures of the moon are conveniently turned around so that they look "right."

What causes this illusion?

We usually see objects illuminated from somewhere above us—very rarely from below. With such overhead illumination a bump on a wall, like a mound on the moon, would appear bright on the upper edge (as shown at A in Fig. 4) and dark on the lower edge (B).

On the other hand, a depression or pit would reveal a bright edge at the bottom (C in Fig. 4) and a dark edge at the top (D).

But consider how the bump and the depression appear when they are illuminated from below. The bright and dark regions reverse, as shown in Fig. 5. The bump takes on the appearance of a depression and vice versa. Thus it is really not easy to distinguish an inverted picture of a relatively unfamiliar object from one that has an unaccustomed direction of illumination.

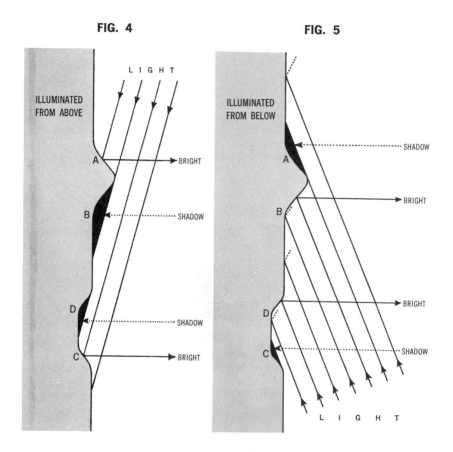

FIG. 4

LIGHT

ILLUMINATED FROM ABOVE

A ► BRIGHT

B ◄ ···· / ············· ·· SHADOW

D ◄ ·········· ········· ·· SHADOW

C ► BRIGHT

FIG. 5

ILLUMINATED FROM BELOW

A ◄ ··········· ··········· SHADOW

B ► BRIGHT

D ► BRIGHT

C ◄ ·········· ·········· ·· SHADOW

LIGHT

This illusion illustrates a fundamental feature of scientific method which might be labeled *Things Are Often Not What They Seem To Be.* The round earth that seems flat, a moving earth that seems still, a relatively stationary sun that seems to move in the sky, solid objects that are mostly empty space, are but a few of the many dramatic examples of this principle.

When a scientist approaches a new problem, one of the first things he must do is to attempt to free himself from the restrictions which his past experience places on the way he will view new events and observations. Of course past experience is valuable as the base upon which new experience is to be evaluated. But a scientist also knows that it will often give him a "mind-set" that prevents him from understanding the things that are really new in the situation. He may see these new events as old ones and perhaps thereby miss a great discovery. The great discoverers were able to free themselves from old habits and thereby chart new ground.

This is the second Puzzle Picture that has been placed upside down. By this time you have probably learned that this is one thing to look for. No doubt you will be turning other photographs around just to make sure that we are not fooling you again. That, too, is part of experiencing scientific method. You are beginning to know the many ways in which the senses and the mind can be fooled. Eventually you will learn to compensate for errors in judgment and thereby become better able to arrive at more accurate conclusions.

III / Observation

We have indicated that the basic starting point for a scientific investigation is the gathering of observations. Sometimes observations of events that occur around us make us wonder about them and this process starts new investigations. Darwin's Theory of Evolution developed in essentially this way as he made his famous voyage around the world on the *Beagle*. Observations gathered on this long trip, plus observations reported by others and recorded in books, provided the factual basis for working out his theory.

Many basic areas of investigation were opened up by accidental observation of events during experiments designed for a totally different purpose. For example, a chance observation by Oersted that current passing through a wire caused a nearby magnetic needle to rotate led to the discovery of electromagnetism and eventually led to such important devices as the telegraph, telephone, electric motor, radio, and television.

Another chance observation by Becquerel, made while he was doing some experiments with phosphorescent materials, led to the discovery of atomic energy, with consequences that he could scarcely have foreseen.

In the Puzzle Picture problems presented in this chapter

you will discover important features of the role that observation plays in scientific discovery and you will note some of the ways in which such observations are used to uncover new information. Keep in mind that we shall deal not only with observation but with the other basic aspects of scientific method as well. In this chapter we merely shift our emphasis slightly to point up the nature of observation.

PUZZLE PICTURE F. RELATING OBSERVATIONS TO PRINCIPLES

This is the same photograph as Puzzle Picture E but turned so that the craters appear as we are accustomed to see them. Let us now examine the details of the features of the moon's landscape. The letters indicate specific features. What questions might you ask about these features?

(PHOTOGRAPH FROM THE MOUNT WILSON AND PALOMAR OBSERVATOR

RELATING OBSERVATIONS TO PRINCIPLES

In many problem situations our observations are guided by basic principles concerning the event or object under investigation.

As an illustration, consider the various features of the moon visible in Puzzle Picture F. By investigating the way in which the sun produces light and dark areas on various types of surface features, we can tell if we are looking at a ridge, a valley, a crater, or a hill. Once the principles of formation of the shadows have been worked out, we can apply them to any set of observations we may make about a particular feature. These principles will also guide us in determining which features to single out for detailed investigation.

To obtain practice in such procedures, suppose you work out the principles of formation of dark and light areas on the moon and then apply them to the following questions:

1. From which direction is the sun shining (right or left)?

2. How does the land slope at A?

3. Is B a hill or a hollow?

4. Is C a hill or a hollow?

5. Describe the nature of the surface at D.

6. Describe the nature of the surface at E.

7. What is the nature of the surface F?

8. In what way does G seem to differ from most of the other craters?

9. Note the craters to the right of the letters H and I. Which has a deeper depression into the crater?

Analysis of Puzzle Picture F

(We suppose that by this time you are thoroughly indoc-

trinated and that you have really tried to answer the questions by yourself.)

Development of principles of the kind we are seeking in this case is often aided substantially by means of diagrams like those shown in Figs. 6 and 7.

Fig. 6 shows the effect of glancing sunlight (K) coming from the right and striking a hill (C). At E the rays are reflected so that most of them go off in the general direction of L and do not reach the observer in the direction of the earth (M). Therefore a level area like that at E will tend to appear gray.

FIG. 6

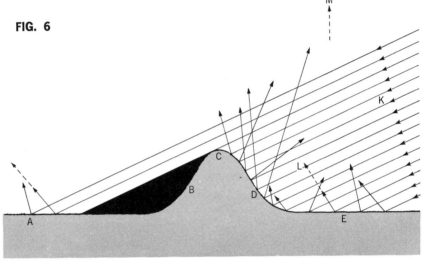

As the surface curves upward at D, more of the rays will bounce off in the direction of the earth (M). Thus the rising slope on the right side of the mountain will appear brighter.

On the other side of the hill at B, light is blocked and produces a black shadow.

56

A depression, such as the one shown at H in Fig. 7, produces the reverse effect. The shadow (at I) appears nearest the source of light. The bright area appears on the side away from the sun (at G). Level areas F and J will appear gray.

FIG. 7

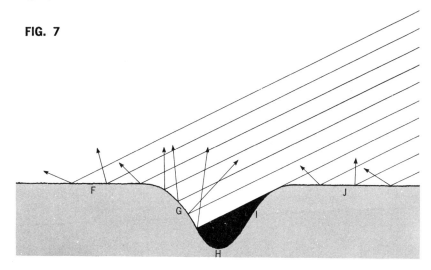

Observe the gradations of tone going across the surface of the moon in the general direction of slanting rays from the sun. These are the principles that will guide our observations:

   a. Shadows appear on the side of a feature away from the sun.
   b. Solid gray areas indicate level regions.
   c. A change from gray to white indicates a rising slope.
   d. A change from white to black indicates a descent from a hill.
   e. A change from gray to black indicates a depression.
   f. An abrupt change from black to white indicates a rise out of a depression.
   g. A change from white to gray indicates a rising slope followed by a level area.

Using these principles as a guide, you can easily determine in some detail the nature of any feature, as indicated in the analysis that follows.

All letter designations in these answers refer to the letters on the Puzzle Picture and not to those in Figs. 6 and 7.

It should be noted that it will not be necessary in all cases to refer back to the principles in a conscious manner. Your mind will often apply the principle so rapidly that you won't be aware that it has been applied. However, the principles will be put to work to guide your observations, whether or not you are aware of it.

1. Shadows appear on the side away from the sun. Since shadows of the crater walls are cast mainly to the left of the wall, the sun must be shining from the right.

2. As we move across A away from the direction of the sun we observe a succession in tone from gray to white to black to gray. According to principles a, b, c, and d this indicates a hill.

3. B is a hill for the same reason as in question 2.

4. C is a depression because we observe a black area followed by white (principle f). However, there is a faint suggestion of a rim because of a slight white area on the right of the circle and a darker area on the left.

5. At D we observe the sequence gray to white to gray. According to principles a, b, c, and g, this indicates a rise from one level area to another; that is, a cliff between two flat regions. There is a level area on the right, a rise, and then the land levels off again beyond the slope at the left.

The fact that there are no shadows seems to indicate that there are no substantial depressions. The gray tone of the land at either side of the bright line indicates that it is level on both sides.

The brightness of the line indicates that the slope faces toward the sun and not away from it.

6. E is a ridge. This is inferred from the length of the line and from the fact that the sequence is: gray, white, black, gray. Principles a, b, c, and d apply here.

7. As we go from right to left across F we observe the sequence: gray, black, white, gray. Applying principles e, f, and g, we see that this sequence would be due to a depression followed by a rise. The length of the depression indicates that it is a long valley.

8. The sharp circular bright area at G that follows the shadow (as one goes from right to left across the diameter of the crater) indicates that there is little or no level floor. A cross-section of the crater resembles a flat "W" in shape. Most of the other craters have level floors.

9. The principles required to answer this question have not been stated. So we must work them out for this special case.

The shadow of the smaller crater at I is longer than that of the larger crater at H. We may therefore infer that the height of the crater wall at I is greater.

One might raise a question about the effect of the roundness of the moon in creating longer shadows. The crater at I is farther from the dark edge of the moon. You may have observed in the photograph that shadows of objects nearer the dark edge tend to be longer. Thus the longer shadow at I indicates even more strongly that the wall is higher there than at H, which is nearer the dark edge.

PUZZLE PICTURE G. IS IT REALLY SO?

Here is still another moon photograph, taken in the Northern Hemisphere. This one shows the apparent motion of the moon in the sky. Put on your thinking cap and give some time to the formulation of questions about this picture.

IS IT REALLY SO?

Many problems in the world are very complex and require a great deal of time, money, and effort to solve. Other problems have not yet been solved despite substantial effort. On the other hand, some questions can be settled with a very simple investigation that may cost almost nothing and take only an hour or two of time.

In solving problems a scientist generally attempts to devise experiments that provide observations dealing with the problem at hand. As a simple illustration of such an experiment, consider the purpose of the photograph on the previous page.

You have observed that when the moon is very low in the sky, it seems to be much larger than when it is overhead. Is this an illusion or is the image really larger? A simple way to answer this question is to use the impartial lens of a camera instead of the easily influenced human eye. Puzzle Picture G provides an objective basis for discovering whether or not the moon's larger appearance near the horizon is an optical illusion.

We shall also ask additional questions that will test your ability to draw conclusions on the basis of observations. Here are the questions:

1. How was this photograph taken?

2. Is the image of the moon really larger than normal when near the horizon?

3. What fact about the atmosphere is revealed by the picture?

4. Is the path of the moon in the sky a straight line or a curve?

5. What are the white dots in the sky?

6. Why isn't the moon in the photograph perfectly round?

7. Is the moon rising or setting?

8. At about what time of night was the picture taken?

9. Did the photographer make any mistakes?

10. You are given the information that the diameter of the moon is about 2,000 miles and its distance from the earth is about 240,000 miles. What inferences may be drawn from these facts and from observation of the photograph?

Analysis of Puzzle Picture G

1. A camera was positioned in one spot and left that way. A picture was then taken while the moon was low in the sky. A few minutes later another picture was taken, with the camera still in the same place and with the exposure the same as before. The background did not change, but the moon's position did. Another image of the moon (second from the bottom) was then recorded on the film.

This process was continued every few minutes until the image of the moon moved out of the limits of the scene. In effect, the line of moons observed in the photograph represents its apparent path through the sky as the earth rotated.

2. Place a sheet of paper across the widest diameter of the lowest image of the moon. Use a fine-pointed pencil to mark off the image diameter on the paper. Then shift the mark to successive images and compare their widest diameters.

You can see that the size of the moon image is certainly not larger near the horizon. In fact, if anything, it seems to be a bit larger higher up.

In the answer to the next question we shall present a possible explanation for the fact that the film may have recorded a larger image higher in the sky.

3. Note that the images of the moon nearer the horizon are darker, while those higher in the sky appear much brighter. This is due to the fact that when the moon is low in the sky, its light passes through the earth's atmosphere at an oblique angle and therefore has to penetrate a much greater thickness of air (Fig. 8). Since air absorbs some light, the more air the light has to pass through the dimmer it becomes.

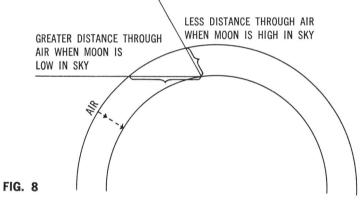

GREATER DISTANCE THROUGH AIR WHEN MOON IS LOW IN SKY

LESS DISTANCE THROUGH AIR WHEN MOON IS HIGH IN SKY

AIR

FIG. 8

The manner in which the light rays bend is affected by the greater thickness of air through which the light must pass when the moon is near the horizon. The amount of bending also depends upon the angle at which the light rays enter the air. As a result, the camera actually records a smaller image of the moon when it is near the horizon. The exact details of the manner in which rays bend is beyond the scope of this book.

4. Place a ruler on the picture and observe that the line does curve a bit.

5. Your first thought may be that the white spots are

63

stars. However, if they were stars they would seem to move in the sky in much the same way that the moon does. Thus each bright star, if it appears in the photograph at all, should appear as a series of white dots in the sky, paralleling the line of moons. Such lines are not observed because the exposures were not long enough to record the dim stars. We may therefore conclude that the white dots are not stars, but something else—probably dust on the negative.

Normally these white dots would be removed from the photograph before it was printed. But this time we let the imperfections remain to make our point.

6. The moon is not perfectly round because it is not exactly at full-moon phase. The upper right portion of the moon seems a bit lopped off. This would indicate that it is slightly beyond the full-moon phase and will thereafter be on the wane (getting smaller each night).

7. The moon is rising because it moves up into the sky from lower left toward upper right. If it were setting, it would descend toward the horizon from upper left to lower right.

8. When the moon is directly opposite the sun, it appears as a full moon in the sky and rises in the east just as the sun sets in the west. Since the moon is just beginning to wane, it must have risen slightly later than a full moon would rise. The almost round shape of the moon tells us that it probably rose within an hour or so of sunset.

9. The photographer slipped up in his timing between the tenth and eleventh image. That interval is slightly larger than the others, as you can verify by measurement with a ruler. He probably made the mistake at that point of delaying the exposure for an extra minute or so.

10. From the given dimensions we can calculate the approximate interval of time between exposures in the photo-

graph. The sky seems to rotate once every twenty-four hours. The time required for the moon to seem to move a distance through the sky equal to its diameter depends upon the ratio of 2,000 miles to the circumference of the large circle shown in Fig. 9. The circumference of a circle is $2\pi r$,

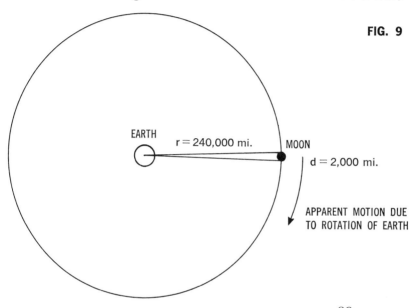

FIG. 9

EARTH

r = 240,000 mi.

MOON

d = 2,000 mi.

APPARENT MOTION DUE TO ROTATION OF EARTH

where r is the radius and π equals approximately $\frac{22}{7}$. Thus the time required for the moon to seem to move to a position one moon diameter away is:

$$\text{Time (in hours)} \quad = \frac{2,000}{2 \times 22 \times 240,000} \times 24$$
$$\frac{}{7}$$

$$\text{Time (in minutes)} = \frac{2,000}{2 \times 22 \times 240,000} \times 24 \times 60$$
$$\frac{}{7}$$

$$= 2 \text{ minutes (approximately)}$$

If the exposures had been taken two minutes apart, the images of the moon would have been just touching each other. Since there is a space of about the width of the moon between images, we can see that the interval between exposures was about four minutes. This figure may be confirmed by more accurate measurements with a ruler and perhaps a magnifying glass or by carefully marking off the moon's diameter several times on the edge of a sheet of paper.

How long did it take to produce the photograph? We count twenty moons. There are nineteen intervals of four minutes each between images. The total time was therefore 19×4 or 76 minutes, or 1 hour and 16 minutes.

Although our original intention was to use the photograph to provide objective evidence about a specific problem, you can see that we have gone rather far afield. The solution of that specific problem was quite simple—just a matter of measuring the diameter of the images of the moon. Yet other observations caught our attention, and each raised a new question. In fact, each of the moon pictures we have used so far in this book has brought forth interesting problems and observations.

That's the way it is in all scientific investigations. An alert person who observes carefully while solving one problem will generally uncover new problems of interest. Some of these may be sufficiently important to warrant further investigation. In this way research in science becomes a never-ending process in which investigation of one problem leads to others.

The areas of knowledge to be explored are probably infinite in extent. Everywhere we look we will find problems to solve. *New problems can be generated by constantly making observations even if they do not bear directly on the problem at hand.* These offshoot observations are the starting points for exploration into the unknown.

66

We also observe in this problem the application of reasoning, measurement, and mathematics. We shall devote special attention to these aspects of scientific method in later chapters.

PUZZLE PICTURE H.   SEARCHING FOR CLUES

This appears to be just an ordinary street scene. What can we possibly want with such a picture? That's for you to discover. Observe this picture carefully and then formulate some interesting questions about it.

SEARCHING FOR CLUES

As your eye wanders over Puzzle Picture H certain general features stand out—buildings, people, cars, shadows, street lamps, trees, a sign, etc. We can stop at each one of these observed features and ask questions about them.

But we can also go beyond the confines of the picture and ask questions about things we cannot see. A question of this kind would be: "Does the building on the right go any higher?" The answer to this question is rather obvious since we see at the top of the photograph only part of a floor and we can infer from our experience that the building just didn't stop right there.

But we can ask more difficult questions about invisible portions of the building and also about its other aspects. For example, we might ask, "How many floors does it have?" or "How many people live in the building?" "When was it built?" etc. Strange as it may seem, it is possible to make observations which, coupled with the application of previous experience and reasoning power, can lead to answers to such questions. Some of the answers may not be exact but may nevertheless be useful.

For example, consider the question, "When was the building erected?" This question directs our attention to a closer observation of the details of architecture. We observe the clean, straight lines, the balconies on each floor, the vents for air conditioners. These observations all point to an apartment house of rather recent construction. We would probably guess that the building was put up after World War II. An architect could probably pinpoint the time more accurately on the basis of his experience with the changes that have occurred in styles of buildings.

Or consider the question, "How many people live in the building?" It may seem that we really can't answer this at all. However, we can set reasonable limits based on experience. We see at least eight floors. This is obviously not a small building. It would be most unreasonable to set ten people as the number who live there. Even a hundred people would seem too low. If we knew the number of floors in the building, we might have a better idea as to the lower limit.

At any rate you can see that even questions that seem impossible to answer can often be investigated to some degree.

The questions that follow are by no means all that you may think of, but they do indicate how observations lead to questions. And in seeking the answers you will have to go back to the photograph to make additional observations that provide clues to the solutions.

Here are the questions:

1. Observe the edge of the building on the right. You cannot see the top. How many floors does it have?

2. How tall is the building (in feet)?

3. What is the season of the year?

4. What is the time of day?

5. Note the light areas in the shadow of the building near the bottom of the picture. Explain how they might have been formed.

Analysis of Puzzle Picture H

1. A clue is provided by the shadow of the building. As you know, shadows conform to the general shape of objects, although there generally are distortions in dimen-

sion. Note the balconies at the extreme left edge of the building at the right. Then observe that the complete shadow of the edge of each is visible on the ground.

Count the number of shadows of balconies. There are twelve. Count the number of floors in the building below where the balconies start. There are five. The total is seventeen.

There is a possibility of an eighteenth floor. Note that above the shadow of the last balcony there is a straight section that seems longer than required for one floor. We can safely assume an extra floor. With the use of a magnifying glass and a ruler we can reasonably establish the existence of that floor.

Note how we have used the processes of observation and deduction to arrive at very specific information about something we cannot see in the photograph. We were able to relate our experience with shadows to our observations of details of the picture. These observations served as clues that enabled us to make deductions about the invisible portion of the building.

As you proceed with other questions in this book, you will note this same process coming into play time and again.

2. We observe drapes, shades, and venetian blinds in the windows of the building. We also note balconies on some of the floors. From these observations we can infer that the building is an apartment house. From experience we know that the ceiling of an average room in new dwellings is about eight feet high.

We can make a rough check by comparing the height of several floors of the building with that of the man walking in the street near it. He is about the same distance from the camera as the building, so we can reasonably use his height for a direct comparison:

$$\frac{\text{Actual height of 5 floors}}{\text{Actual height of man}} = \frac{\text{Height of 5 floors in picture}}{\text{Height of man in picture}}$$

Measure the height of the man in the photograph with a ruler. It is seen to be 1.3 cm. Measure the height of the first five floors (street to first balcony). It is 9.8 cm. What shall we assume the height of the man to be? The average man is about 5 ft. 10 in. tall. Assume 6 ft. for a moderately tall man.

$$\frac{H}{6 \text{ ft.}} = \frac{9.8 \text{ cm.}}{1.3 \text{ cm.}}$$

$$H = \frac{9.8 \times 6}{1.3}$$

$$= 45 \text{ ft. (height of 5 floors)}$$

The height of one floor is then $\frac{1}{5} \times 45$ ft., or 9 ft. Considering the rough nature of the measurements, this is fairly close to the approximate 8-ft. height of a floor.

Let's assume a height of 5 ft. 6 in. for a short man. Then the calculation is:

$$\frac{H}{5\frac{1}{2} \text{ ft.}} = \frac{9.8}{1.3}$$

$$H = 41.5 \text{ ft.}$$

The height of one floor is then $\frac{1}{5} \times 41.5$, or 8.3 ft. The 8-ft. height now seems to be a more reasonable selection.

It is interesting to note that if our measurements are accurate we have a clue about the height of the man. When we assumed the man to be short, our ceiling height turned out to be probably too low. Of course the measurements and estimates are so rough that we cannot make them more than approximations.

We might seek another "yardstick." You could use a magnifying glass and count the number of bricks in one floor. Then you might inquire at a building-supply company about the size of bricks. You may well get a very accurate height that way. If the problem were sufficiently important, you might go to that trouble.

At any rate, assuming the height of a floor to be about 8 ft., we obtain for the height of the 18-story building:

$$H = 18 \times 8 \text{ ft.}$$
$$= 144 \text{ ft.}$$

There is an important feature of scientific method shown here. When making inferences about unknown actions, events, and objects, we try to increase the probability that we are correct by approaching the problem by means of several different methods. In this case the key to a more accurate answer is the height of the floor. Our attention is then focused on estimating the height in several different ways.

3. A clue to the season of the year is sought by looking for characteristics related to season. The people in the streets are wearing jackets, not overcoats or shirts. So the likelihood is that it is not winter or summer (although it might be).

Several small trees are visible. They have leaves that seem rather small. This fact would make us inclined to favor early spring. However, we must put this down as just a likelihood. We wouldn't rate this guess as being highly probable.

4. The shadows provide a clue to the time of day. They seem too long to be noon shadows in spring in most latitudes of the United States. They are definitely too short to occur very early in the morning or evening. A probable time would be mid-morning or mid-afternoon. However, there is a possibility that the shadows would be appropriate for noontime on a warm winter day in the northern part of the United States.

You will recall our "no holds barred" approach to problems. It would be perfectly fair to take a magnifying glass and go hunting for a clock somewhere in the photograph. There is one just to the right of the flag near the far street corner. Perhaps you would like to see if you could obtain the time that way.

5. We added this question to the list to show how new problems can arise from careful observation coupled with curiosity. The shadow in the ramp leading to the parking area is obviously that of a building, probably the one from which the photographer took the picture. The lighter strips in the shadow indicate that additional light is coming from somewhere.

One possibility is a reflection of the sun. The regularity of the light areas and the way they line up point to the windows of the apartment building as the source.

(U.S. AIR FO▉

PUZZLE PICTURE I. FORMING PATTERNS

There seems to be a great deal of to-do around this giant radome (radar dome) at Tyngsboro, Massachusetts. It looks as though the finishing touches are being applied to the dome. But that's not what interests us most. Can you pose some questions of a different sort?

FORMING PATTERNS

To illustrate the way in which a confusing jumble of facts is put into scientific order, let us consider the seemingly haphazard triangles observed on the outer surface of the sphere in Puzzle Picture I. What seems to be a disorganized jumble probably has some kind of pattern, since it is difficult to believe that the engineers designed it to be a jumble. What was their plan of construction? What geometrical patterns were used in making this sphere?

Among the basic requirements for working out such a pattern are: careful observation, adequate time, and concentrated thought.

A first glance gives the overall picture—the spherical shape, the men on top, the crane, men on a suspended platform, the building below the sphere, people and cars on the ground, and the surrounding trees.

Now fix your eyes on the triangles. Let your eyes run over the lines and arcs of triangles. Look for familiar shapes: squares, rectangles, rhombuses (diamond shapes), pentagons, hexagons, etc. Try to locate *regular* shapes (with sides of equal length and with equal angles between them). Some common shapes you might seek are shown in Fig. 10.

It is helpful to use a transparent sheet of some kind over the picture. Trace the shapes you find on the surface of the sheet with a soft pencil or crayon. Be sure not to mark the page of the book itself.

And let us remind you to spend some time on this problem before you look for the pattern in the following pages.

Analysis of Puzzle Picture I

Perhaps the most noticeable features at first glance are the almost circular polygons centering at A in Fig. 11. (A

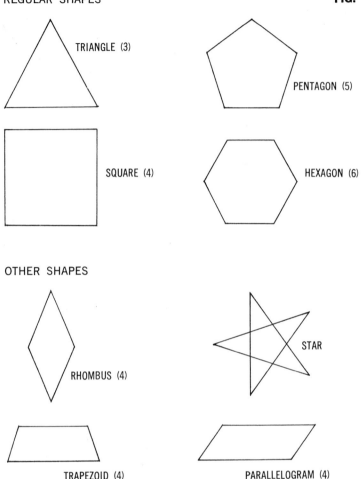

REGULAR SHAPES

TRIANGLE (3)

PENTAGON (5)

SQUARE (4)

HEXAGON (6)

OTHER SHAPES

RHOMBUS (4)

STAR

TRAPEZOID (4)

PARALLELOGRAM (4)

FIG. 10

polygon is a closed figure composed of straight sides.) Both polygons are regular. The one at B has nine equal sides. The one at C has fifteen equal sides.

A similar set of polygons is observed to center at D. There are others at E, F, G, H, and K.

The centers of these polygons with nine and fifteen sides are on the points of a regular pentagon (ADEFG). Note

FIG. 11

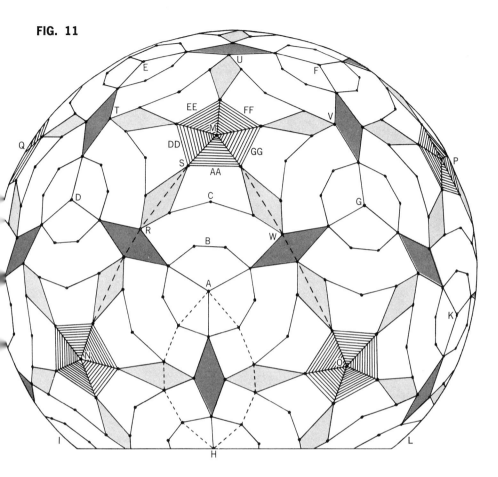

that the fifteen-sided polygons touch each other. Each has one side in common with another that it touches.

By extending this pattern in all directions similar pentagons are observed around the sphere with centers at or near M, N, O, P, and H. A portion of one such pentagon starts at ED and goes over to the other side of the sphere at the upper left. Another, at EF, goes over the top. Still another starts at FGK and goes around to the other side at the upper right. A small portion of yet another one starts at KL and goes out of sight at the lower right.

There is a solid shape known as a regular *dodecahedron* (Fig. 12), which is composed of twelve regular pentagons. Note that this solid shape approximates a sphere. Actually its *vertices* (corner points) lie on the surface of a sphere. Note the great resemblance between the regular dodecahedron and the large pentagons in the radome pattern. It seems clear that the engineers designing this radome based their construction on this dodecahedron pattern.

Now observe that at the center of each large pentagon there is a smaller one. For example, pentagon ADEFG (Fig. 11) has its center at M. Note the small pentagon around M. Side AA corresponds to point A, DD to D, EE to E, FF to F, and GG to G. Other pentagons of this type are observed at N and O. Part of such a pentagon is observed at P.

Imagine a large equilateral (equal-sided) triangle connecting M, N, and O. Another is seen joining M, O, and P. Other large triangles are formed by a) M, N, and the center of another pentagon out of sight near Q; b) P, O, and a point out of sight beyond K; c) O, N, and a point out of sight beyond H.

The regular *icosahedron* (Fig. 13) is a solid shape with

FIG. 12   **FIG. 13**

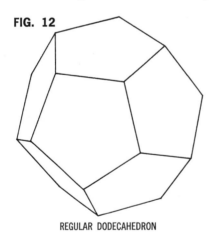

REGULAR DODECAHEDRON

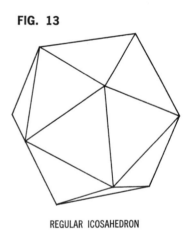

REGULAR ICOSAHEDRON

twenty equilateral triangles making up an approximately spherical solid. The vertices of these triangles all lie on a sphere. Note the resemblance between the icosahedron and the radome's pattern of triangles just described.

Next observe the rhombuses (diamond shapes) shown with dark shading in Fig. 11. Observe how each rhombus connects two of the nine-sided polygons and has as a diagonal the common side of two fifteen-sided polygons. Also observe that the connecting links between the centers (A and G) of the nine-sided and fifteen-sided polygons are composed of a line, a rhombus, and another line.

There are patterns of quadrilaterals (four-sided figures) like the one connecting R and S. These are shown in light shading. Note that each of these is part of a five-sided shape, such as RTUVW. Observe that each connecting line between pentagon centers (such as M and N) is composed of a line, a quadrilateral, a line, a quadrilateral, and a line.

This should suffice to answer our question adequately for our purposes. But why not continue a bit yourself? Are there any other relationships you can discover?

Here is one suggestion. Investigate the nature of the arcs connecting centers of the nine-sided polygons. Two such arcs are shown with dotted lines from A to H.

This Puzzle Picture illustrates the manner in which a scientist can bring order out of apparent chaos. Many observations of objects and events at first appear to present a confusing jumble. That seems to be the case with the arrangement of triangles on the radome. A similar confusing variety and jumble are the first impressions one gets when observing the many varieties of plants, animals, rocks, minerals, fossils, and stars that we encounter in our experience.

Scientists constantly strive to discover patterns that tie

observations together and organize them into neat, meaningful bundles that can be handled more efficiently. *Such organized patterns lead to deeper understanding of the fundamental nature of the events or objects being observed.*

Our analysis of Puzzle Picture I illustrates in a simple manner how we go about gathering observations to create patterned order out of apparent chaos.

IV / Scientific Reasoning

Observations, by themselves, would prove rather barren in producing new knowledge and solving problems. But when these observations are used as the basis for reasoning, then their partnership becomes very fruitful indeed. All of modern science has arisen from this partnership. An important part of this process has been the use of experiments for making observations and testing the results of reasoning.

In previous Puzzle Picture problems we have used reasoning in connection with observation, but with the stress on what we could learn about the observation. In this chapter we shall continue to use both observation and reasoning, but this time we shall explore more deeply what we can learn about reasoning.

(WIDE WORLD PHC

PUZZLE PICTURE J.   TESTING HYPOTHESES

It may seem strange to include a photograph of six beautiful young ladies in a book on scientific method. What could there possibly be to discover here? Put on your thinking cap and formulate some questions about this picture.

TESTING HYPOTHESES

In Chapter 1 we noted that in scientific investigations hypotheses are suggested and theories are developed to explain observations. It is essential to test an hypothesis or a theory to discover whether or not it is correct. As an illustration, consider the problem of "spontaneous generation." In the past it was believed that flies and other insects came from decaying meat or other refuse. It was thought that they came from the meat spontaneously (by themselves) without any participation by adult flies or insects. There was good evidence for this belief in the common observation that flies came from tiny, wormlike creatures called maggots, which in turn seemed to arise spontaneously from the decaying meat.

In 1668 an Italian scientist, Francesco Reti, wondered about this. He observed that adult flies were attracted by decaying meat. Perhaps they were responsible in some unknown way for the later appearance of maggots and young flies. Reti's hypothesis could be stated as follows: "Young flies do not come by themselves from decaying meat but require the participation of adult flies in some manner."

At that time this hypothesis was no better than the one based upon spontaneous generation. The only way to decide between the two views was to gather observations. By far the best type of observation in such a case is one that comes from a controlled experiment. Reti went about it this way: He placed decaying meat in a number of containers and covered some of them with gauze, leaving the others open. No flies could reach the meat in the covered containers, but the insects could easily alight on the meat in the uncovered ones.

The hypothesis of spontaneous generation predicted that

flies should develop in both types of containers. Reti's hypothesis led to the prediction that maggots would develop only in the uncovered containers. Each hypothesis would stand or fall on the outcome of an actual series of trials.

In his experiment Reti observed that flies were attracted to the meat in both types of containers, but actually touched the meat only in the uncovered ones. Afterwards maggots and young flies developed in the uncovered containers and not in those covered by gauze.

Reti could have performed many different kinds of experiments with flies, but the one he selected *tested* the predictions that were made from both hypotheses. It provided a conclusive test of which idea was true and which false. Of course one can raise objections to the way the experiment was performed and perhaps try other experiments to meet these objections. But for our purposes we can consider Reti's experiment to be close to proof that his hypothesis was true and the accepted one of spontaneous generation false.

Strange as it may seem, the photograph of the young ladies will help us to illustrate this process of testing hypotheses.

You may have observed in Puzzle Picture J that the three young ladies on the left have a striking resemblance to the three on the right. The question naturally arises as to why this resemblance occurs. A possible explanation comes to mind. Perhaps this is a picture of three sets of identical twins. That statement is an hypothesis, *a guess at a possible explanation.* Of course this is not any guess taken out of thin air, but is based on our experience and our observations of the photograph. But even if the hypothesis "works" in the sense that it explains our observation, that does not prove that it is really correct.

We can think of another hypothesis to explain the same observation. Perhaps three young ladies are looking into a mirror. Then their images would *appear* to be those of identical twins. Certainly that is as good an explanation as the one about identical twins.

Now which one is correct? To settle that question we must devise some kind of test to distinguish between both hypotheses. We will have to consider the basic principles involved in this situation and reason from these principles. Then we will devise experiments and make predictions. Finally we will perform these experiments and gather appropriate observations that will provide the basis for making judgments about the truth or falsity of each hypothesis.

The reasoning process in this case follows a kind of "experiment in the mind" wherein we imagine certain things to be the case and then follow up their consequences mentally according to principles we already know.

Can you apply your knowledge and reasoning power to devise one or more tests that will enable you to distinguish between the hypothesis of three sets of identical twins and that of three girls looking into a mirror?

Analysis of Puzzle Picture J

For the moment let us consider the consequences of the hypothesis that Puzzle Picture J shows three sets of identical twins, and not a mirror image. In that case we could put it to the test by seeking some way in which the paired "twins" appeared different from each other. For example, if we could find a mole on the cheek of one girl and no corresponding mole on her "twin" then we would have strong evidence that the photograph does not show a mirror image. Conversely, in a mirror image we would have to find *every* feature of the girl duplicated in the mirror.

The matter is complicated in this case because the positions of the girls and their images are in different places. So we get different views of the girls and their images.

First, note that the smiles on each correspond very closely with the smiles of their "twins" or mirror images. This makes us lean toward the mirror hypothesis. But then, perhaps the photographer had this in mind and purposely set up the picture to make it look like a mirror image. Perhaps that is the whole point of the picture. So let's gather additional observations.

An important property of mirrors is that all images are located as far back of the mirror as the object is in front. Also, image and object are always on a line perpendicular to the mirror.

These facts are portrayed in Fig. 14. Three "object"

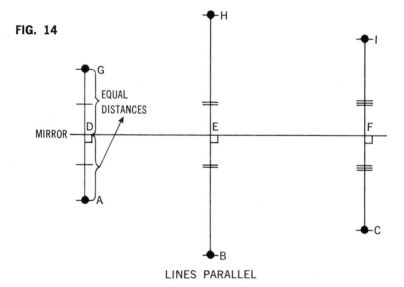

FIG. 14

LINES PARALLEL

points (A, B, C) are shown. To locate the image for one of the objects we draw a perpendicular line from the object to the mirror. The three perpendicular lines are AD, BE, and CF. Each of these lines is then extended an equal distance behind the mirror to the image points (G, H, I).

Note that the lines connecting objects and images (AG, BH, CI) are all parallel to each other because they are all perpendicular to the same line. This provides a test for distinguishing between a mirror image and identical twins. If the lines joining related points on the photograph are all parallel to each other, then the evidence will be very strong—practically conclusive—that the picture shows a mirror image. It seems very unlikely that a photographer could set up a situation in which three sets of identical twins are placed so that they are exactly where a mirror image would seem to be.

How do parallel lines in a three-dimensional situation appear on a two-dimensional photograph? As you know, they seem to converge to a point, just as two parallel railroad tracks appear to converge at a distance. So we can be reasonably certain that lines are parallel in the original scene if they converge to a point on the photograph.

This, then, is our crucial test. If the lines connecting corresponding points on the photograph converge to a point, then we can be fairly sure that we are viewing a mirror image. If we find even one that does not converge to the same point as the others, then we can reject the mirror hypothesis.

Place a piece of transparent material on the photograph and mark off corresponding points, as shown in Fig. 15. Then carefully extend each line until it meets the others. Fig. 15 shows that the lines converge to a point approximately in the region EF.

FIG. 15

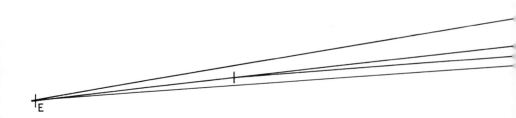

Considering the difficulties involved in making this drawing, points E and F are sufficiently close so that we can reasonably conclude that the lines converge to approximately
a point. In that case we can also conclude that the picture
is that of three girls and a mirror image.

But observe that the convergence is not exact. This raises
the question of whether or not the measurement is exact
enough for our purposes. Obviously there is still a slight
possibility that the mirror hypothesis is not correct, and
only further measurement and observation will narrow
down the range of error.

Actually, the same sort of thing happens with all tests.
We can never measure absolutely exactly. No matter how
much care we take, there is always a certain small margin
of error. As a result, it is impossible ever to be *absolutely*
sure about any test or observation. All we can do is estimate the probability that we are right. This also means
that we must always keep our minds open to the possibility
that we are wrong.

In Fig. 15 we could investigate the matter more carefully by selecting additional points for drawing lines, by
making more exact measurements using a magnifying glass

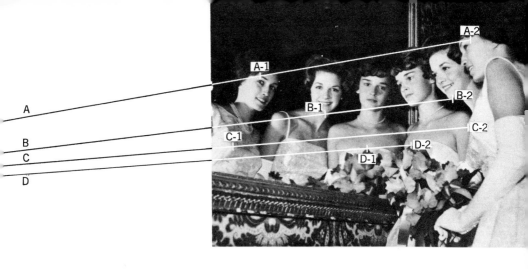

or microscope, by attempting to make corrections for errors that the camera may have introduced and perhaps in other ways. These steps are all characteristic of scientific method.

Several additional aspects of scientific method are revealed through this Puzzle Picture. First, care was taken to mark positions of equivalent points as accurately as possible. A long metal ruler was therefore used to ensure straight lines. (Fig. 15 is reduced from the original drawing used for measurement.) Second, to be objective one must not look at where the lines are going as the straight edge is being positioned on the marks. This tends to prejudice the placement of the ruler to make the line "come out right." If the lines really meet without such adjustment, one can be fortified in the opinion that the hypothesis of a mirror image is being proved. If the position of the ruler is altered even a little by the experimenter in his desire to prove a point, then the test breaks down. In other words, *complete honesty in carrying out the experiment is essential for it to be any guide to the truth.*

Third, *contrary evidence must not be suppressed.* This feature is observed in connection with line C in Fig. 15.

Although it passes through the same general area that the others do, it stands out as the only one that does not meet the others in a very small region near E. In such a situation most people have a tendency to suppress the evidence here, because it may seem obvious that it "doesn't belong." It would be a good idea to investigate this one line more thoroughly to find out why it stood out in this way. It may have been misplaced because of a slightly inaccurate placement of the original marks, or a small error in drawing of the line or perhaps a defect in the mirror. On the other hand, the displacement may indicate something fundamentally wrong with the hypothesis.

We shall not investigate further at this stage because we have made our basic point. But you may wish to pursue the matter with additional observations and experiments.

PUZZLE PICTURE K.   FINDING CONTRADICTIONS

What questions might we ask about the girl's discovery?

FINDING CONTRADICTIONS

In Puzzle Picture K we turn for a moment from photographs to study a comic strip. The aspect of scientific method that we wish to illustrate is the way a scientist goes about disproving statements that seem to have some plausibility. The girl's statements might be true. Some clever inventor may have invented a bag that magnifies potatoes. But if you were a scientist how would you analyze the situation?

Here are your questions:

1. What contradictions can you find in the statements or drawings?

2. Could a plastic bag be made that would magnify the potatoes as Nancy claims?

Analysis of Puzzle Picture K

1. No matter how the bag magnified the appearance of the potatoes their actual volume would not be altered. So in an actual situation the small potatoes shown in the last panel would fall to the bottom of the bag and leave the top flabby and loose. It would then be obvious that the bag was only partly filled.

However, the potatoes in the bag in the second panel seem to fill up the bag completely. This would not happen in a real situation, even if the bag could magnify their appearance.

The artist has purposely distorted the drawings to lead the reader to accept the point of the cartoon as plausible. He has made the potatoes very much smaller in the fourth panel than in the second. This is a contradiction between the cartoon and reality that casts doubt on the cartoon's validity. *Pointing out such a contradiction is one of the main ways in which a scientist seeks to disprove a statement.*

Another contradiction, but one which is not as obvious as the one noted above, involves practical experience with the way potatoes are sold. They are usually sold by the pound, not by their apparent size. The grocer would be a "gyp" if he sold a five-pound bag of potatoes at a higher-than-usual price. Of course that may be the case, but the cartoon implies that the girl is complaining about the size of the potatoes, not their total weight. Even if the size were magnified, the grocer would not be considered a "gyp" unless the price of the potatoes per pound were also raised.

2. Let us now consider the physical problem of producing magnification in a flat plastic bag. This involves some knowledge of the way a lens acts.

There are two ways in which an image formed by light can be magnified. One way is by means of a convex lens (one that is thickest in the middle). The other way is by means of concave mirrors. We can rule out concave mirrors because a mirror would have to be opaque to light coming from the other side. So it would no longer look like a clear bag from both sides. Also the bag would have to be rigid so that the curvature of the mirror was maintained.

Let us consider the possibility of a lens system. Fig. 16 shows what such a bag looks like. There is a convex lens at A. Such a lens would need substantial thickness of plastic to be convex enough to magnify. This would make the plastic bag thick, heavy, and costly. The likelihood of such a bag being practical is very slim.

Moreover there would be little point in having only one side magnify, since the deception would be revealed if the customer turned the bag over. So another lens (B) would probably have to be put on the other side of the bag.

Perhaps the bag could be made of a series of very small lenses as shown in Fig. 17. There is one lens from A to C,

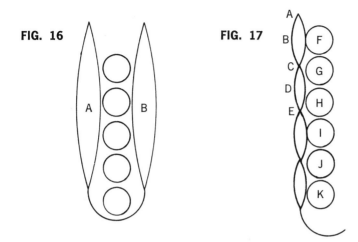

FIG. 16

FIG. 17

another from C to E, etc. A potato or part of a potato at F— near the thick parts of a lens—might appear magnified when viewed from outside. But notice the parts of the lenses near C and E. The bag can't bulge outward in a convex manner everywhere. At C and E the bulge reverses, and changes to a concave (thinner) region of the plastic. And the effect of a concave part is just the reverse of the convex part. It "minifies" instead of magnifying. Since the lenses are small, the overall effect will be for the potato to appear of normal size, but with some parts appearing larger and others smaller.

Moreover as a person moves about in the store different parts would be magnified and "minified." As a result it would be quite obvious to the customers that the bag is not just a simple thin plastic but some special kind of bag.

There is a type of lens known as a "Fresnel lens," whose surface consists of "steps" of thicker plastic that give the impression of flatness. But such lenses would still show the same "minifying" effect where the different lenses meet.

Also, as described earlier, the actual volume of the potatoes would not be altered, and if there really were fewer than the normal number of potatoes or the same number of smaller potatoes, part of the bag would have no potatoes back of it. In that case the lenses would distort the view of objects seen through the bag. So it would no longer look like a normal flat bag, but a special one, obviously with lenses of some kind. The customer would really not be fooled.

With this kind of reasoning we have shown that:

a. Such a bag is not practical.

b. It would not do what the cartoon implies it would.

c. According to our knowledge of lenses it would not be possible to make a bag that could do what is claimed.

For all these reasons we can conclude that the situation portrayed in the cartoon most probably could not really occur.

Of course, as pointed out many times before, we must not make this conclusion an absolutely certain one. Despite all we may say some scientist may one day discover new principles of optics that might be applied to making such a magnifying bag. But it isn't likely that the cartoonist knows about such principles. Nor is he concerned about whether or not his cartoon can be true or not. He is just interested in a plausible situation that makes us laugh. It would be wrong of us to take his fun away and we are grateful to him for providing us with a lesson in scientific reasoning.

Analyses of the kind we have made in this situation are an important part of scientific method. *Any scientist who develops a theory has to try to punch holes in it the way we have done. If he finds too many serious contradictions, he must be prepared to junk his theory. If he doesn't, other scientists will. Only if a theory can withstand such assaults in the search for contradictions can it survive and be accepted as likely to be true.*

If this kind of reasoned analysis and contradiction-finding is applied to everyday situations, it can cause a great deal of enmity and hard feelings. People are just not trained to search for contradictions or to welcome them, even if they are sincerely made. Yet to be really scientific one must not only welcome such analyses by others but one should also be in the forefront of the search for contradictions. A good scientist should analyze his own work mercilessly before he presents it to other scientists. Otherwise he is not a scientist and will be so criticized by others.

(COURTESY OF THE AMERICAN MUSEUM OF NATURAL HISTORY)

PUZZLE PICTURE L.
REASONING FROM OBSERVATIONS

This photograph shows a portion of the cross-section of a tree. Only half of the cross-section is shown so that you can count rings more easily. We needn't tell you that one of the questions will obviously deal with the age of the tree at the time it was cut down. But that's really too simple a question for a careful observer. There are more subtle problems here which you will discover by means of careful observation. See if you can list several such problems.

REASONING FROM OBSERVATIONS

Here are some questions you might ask about Puzzle Picture L:

1. How old was the tree when it was cut down?

2. Why are the rings off center, with the greater thicknesses toward the bottom of the picture?

3. As we look outward from the center we observe that the rings become very closely spaced at a certain point, then very much farther apart or wider, and once again very narrow near the outer portion. What might have happened to the tree to cause such differences?

Analysis of Puzzle Picture L

1. As you probably know, the age of a tree can usually be determined by the number of rings in its trunk. We can count 23 rings in section A (Fig. 18), including the center as one ring. The rings in layer B are difficult to count, but we can estimate about 8.

These are followed by 16 wide rings (C) and then by about 9 narrow ones.

The total number of rings is about $23 + 8 + 16 + 9$, or 56. This indicates an age of 56 years at the time of cutting.

2. We would expect the tree to grow in an even manner all around. The rings should be circles, all with the same center. What hypotheses can we offer to explain the consistently greater growth on one side?

Perhaps the side facing the sun grows more rapidly, or vice versa. A moment's thought would cause us to reject this explanation as probably incorrect. A tree has branches and leaves on all sides. Sunlight would produce sugar in all of these leaves equally. Then the sugar would probably be distributed equally to all parts of the trunk.

FIG. 18

Of course this hypothesis is easily subject to check by observation of trees. Normal tree trunks do show approximately equal growth in all directions with the rings appearing as approximate circles having the same center.

There must be some factor causing more growth on one side.

Perhaps the tree was leaning. This would imply that one side would have to be stronger and thicker to oppose the forces tending to bend the tree downward. A reasonable hypothesis would be that the side leaning toward the ground would be different in thickness than the upper side.

This hypothesis has been checked by observation of leaning trees and has been found to be correct.

So the tree in our Puzzle Picture probably started out in life leaning in one direction and this caused the uneven development of its rings. However, we must keep in mind that there may be other factors at work in this case, which a more careful study might reveal.

3. If rings are the result of growth, it seems reasonable to infer that wide rings occur during years of rapid growth, while narrow rings develop during years of little growth. If this is true (and it is), we can infer that the rings in sections A and C were periods of rapid growth while the rings in sections B and D represented periods when growth was slow.

It is then natural to inquire as to what may have caused poor growth. Among the factors that may come to mind are: drought, disease, insect attack, deprivation of light by other trees, injury or breakage of limbs. An expert can often tell from the appearance of the rings and from the history of the region what the cause of the periods of slow growth may have been.

From the above discussion we can infer the life history of the tree to be:

Period A: (age 0–23)—23 years of rapid growth, but with the tree starting out leaning to one side. The tree continues to lean in that direction all its life.

Period B: (age 24–31)—8 years of slow growth, with some pestilence or other obstacle to growth.

Period C: (age 32–47)—16 years of extremely rapid growth, as shown by the very wide rings in section C. Perhaps the tree became tall enough to reach sunlight directly, whereas in previous years it was partially covered by taller trees. Or the more rapid growth may have occurred because the tree was larger and able to produce much more food for itself.

Period D: (age 48–56)—9 years of very slow growth. The tree was probably affected by some disease or damage by insects. Obviously the tree was cut down at the end of this period.

The analysis of this Puzzle Picture illustrates a fundamental way in which information is obtained by scientists. *A connection is discovered between two separate types of events by means of careful observation. Then this connection is used as the basis for making deductions, generalizations and hypotheses. These deductions, generalizations, and hypotheses then suggest investigations by means of additional observations or experiments.* Such investigations generally enlarge our knowledge of the subject and in turn lead to new questions and directions for investigation.

When you stop to think of it, our discussion of the life history of the tree was based on relatively few observations of the tree trunk. It takes only a few minutes to arrive at a reasonable life history of the tree just by counting some dark and light rings in a cross-section of its trunk. This indicates the power of a fact or a principle that connects two separate types of events. In this case the connection is made between dark and light rings and passage of time.

It should be noted that the original principle that a ring in the trunk of a tree is associated with a year of growth probably took mankind a long time to discover. But once discovered and made known to many people, it becomes a powerful tool for deriving new knowledge.

As another illustration, consider the very similar powerful tool for discovery of the life history of the earth from the layers of sedimentary rock found in many parts of the earth. A geologist who understands the principles of formation of rock from sediments can go into a region and deduce its "life history" by studying the way the different sedimentary layers were deposited in ancient seas and by observing the types of fossils found in each layer. The thickness of the layers and the fossils found in them provide some clues to the time when the rock layers were formed.

You will find similar methods of discovering new information not only in science, but in all areas of human activity. A good businessman will operate his business on the basis of similar principles which he has learned by experience, from other businessmen, or perhaps at school. Today, as knowledge about running a business is accumulated, the tendency is to transmit these principles in organized form through college courses. Although some people might object to our saying so, this development indicates the possibility that business management may one day become a science, in somewhat the same sense that physics, geology, or biology are now considered sciences.

PUZZLE PICTURE M.   MAKING DEDUCTIONS FROM OBSERVATIONS

We doubt if you will have much trouble posing an interesting question or two about this picture.

MAKING DEDUCTIONS FROM OBSERVATIONS

As we have seen, we must be deeply concerned about a contradiction to an accepted fact because this implies that there is some new, underlying factor at work. Discovery of such a hidden factor sometimes leads to important new knowledge and invention. So a good scientist never ignores a contradiction but seeks to resolve it by probing more deeply into the situation.

The contradiction that confronts us in Puzzle Picture M is the appearance of a curved propeller. We know from experience that propellers are straight. Or if this is a special propeller, we would expect both blades to curve symmetrically and not in the unbalanced manner shown in the photograph.

Your questions, then, are:

1. Why does the propeller appear curved?

2. Why does the blade appear much thicker on the left side of the picture than on the right?

Analysis of Puzzle Picture M

(We know that this is a difficult problem that involves some practical knowledge of photography. So if you are not familiar with photography, we will let you read the next four paragraphs. Then you must promise to stop reading and start thinking.)

You know that a fast-moving object produces a blur on a photograph because the light is allowed to enter for a definite time. During that time the object moves and its image also moves on the film. The extent of the blur indicates the amount of motion during the time the lens was open.

The less expensive cameras have "shutters" near the lens.

The shutter opens, lets light in to reach all parts of the film almost simultaneously, and then rapidly closes. With such a shutter near the lens both blades of a propeller would appear equally blurred on a photograph.

More expensive cameras have what is called "focal plane shutters." Fig. 19 shows the film (ABCD) at the back of a camera with such a shutter in front of it. The shutter is a black opaque cloth (EF) in front of the film. When the button is pressed, an open slit (GH) in the cloth rapidly moves across the entire front of the film, exposing one small bit of the film at a time as it goes.

FIG. 19

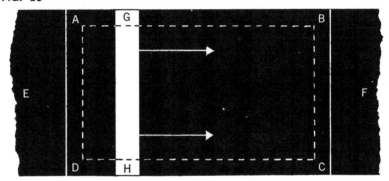

Such an arrangement makes it possible to "stop" motion on the film more effectively than with other types of shutters. Shorter exposure times are possible. But you can also see that the part of the film near AD receives light before the portions near BC.

(Now stop reading and return to thinking about the problem. Look at the explanation that follows only after attempting to answer the questions by yourself.)

Let us see what effect such an arrangement would have on a spinning propeller. In Fig. 20–*1*, AB represents the

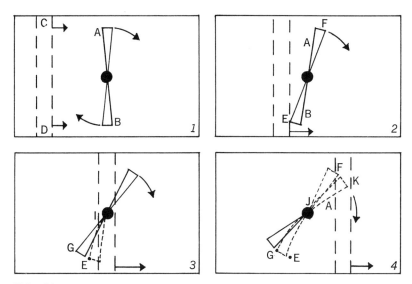

FIG. 20

image of a propeller on the back of a camera. The image is turning in the direction shown by the curved arrows. Assume that the slit (CD) is moving toward the image of the propeller. Let us break the sequence of events into small steps as shown in the four separate panels (1, 2, 3, 4).

In panel 2 the image of the propeller has turned a bit while the slit moved closer. The slit begins to pass in front of the image of blade B. The tip of the blade (E) will now begin to be recorded on the film as the slit passes by. The image of the portion of the blade at A is not yet recorded on the film. Since the slit and the blade are moving toward each other, they will pass each other more rapidly than if the blade were still.

In panel 3 the slit is passing the center of the image of the propeller. In the meantime the image of the tip has moved from E to G. But G is no longer exposed. So position E is the one recorded on the film. But now the position

105

of the blade at I is pointing toward G. So the film appears as a curve from E to I, instead of a straight line.

Because of the motion, the image will be blurred. Also, since the outer tip of the blade covers a bigger circle than the parts near the center in the same time, it is moving faster and therefore appears more blurred.

In panel 4 the slit has moved farther to the right. At the same time the tip of blade A has moved from F to K. However, the portion of the blade near the center (J) was pointing toward F at the time the slit passed by. So the blade appears curved from J to K. Our reasoning shows that the image of the entire propeller would appear as a curve instead of a straight line. This explains our observation of a curved propeller in this Puzzle Picture.

There is also an important difference between the way the images of blades A and B are passed by the slit. The image of blade A moves in the same direction as the slit, while B moves in the opposite direction. Therefore blade A lingers in the area of the slit while being overtaken by it. Blade B is passed more quickly because it is moving in the opposite direction.

This point can be illustrated more clearly by comparing the situation with two automobiles passing each other. Suppose one car is going 50 miles an hour and the other 30. If they pass in opposite directions the relative speed is 50 plus 30, or 80 miles an hour. They zoom past each other very quickly. But if one is overtaking the other in the same direction the relative speed is 50 minus 30, or 20 miles an hour. It will then require a much longer time for the cars to pass each other.

From this reasoning it follows that the blade moving in the same direction as the slit should appear more blurred.

This explains why one end of the blade in the photograph appears much more blurred than the other.

Now, there is a loophole in our reasoning. We made certain assumptions about the position of the propeller in relation to the slit. Suppose we had assumed that the propeller was perpendicular to the slit at the start instead of being parallel to it, as shown in Fig. 21? You can employ the same kind of reasoning as before to show that the propeller will be curved as shown by the dotted area in Fig. 21. We leave that for you to pursue.

FIG. 21

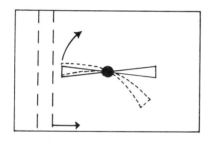

We have explained the observations in the photograph. But how do we know that the explanation is right? You may be interested in considering this problem. If so, let us point out some interesting directions.

The amount of curvature of the blade and the way in which both ends blur will depend upon how rapidly the propeller is rotating and how fast the focal plane shutter is moving. It probably also depends upon the width of the slit opening. Furthermore it will make a difference if the slit is moving from right to left, or from left to right, or up, or down. It should be possible to analyze these situations for different positions and speeds of the propeller. Such an analysis would probably enable one to figure out, from the appearance of the photograph, what conditions produced it. This type of analysis might prove to be an interesting new way of measuring high-speed rotation. Using a Polaroid-type camera one could take a quick photograph of a rotating object, make suitable measurements on the photograph, and then use this information to calculate the speed of rotation. Or if the speed of rotation were known, one might be able to check the speed of the shutter.

What we are suggesting is a new invention—a practical application of a scientific principle. This would make a most interesting science project for an enterprising reader.

This Puzzle Picture illustrates how:

a. We can make deductions about events we cannot see by observing and studying the effects they produce.

b. Contradictions to our experience give rise to new problems that lead to the discovery of hidden causes.

c. Discovery of the causes of events often enables us to make useful predictions and create new inventions.

d. We must constantly examine the assumptions we have made during a reasoning process to be sure that we have not omitted important factors that would affect our conclusions.

e. Drawings are useful in enabling us to reason about the hidden causes of events.

f. Reasoning and observation both play a basic role in deriving new knowledge.

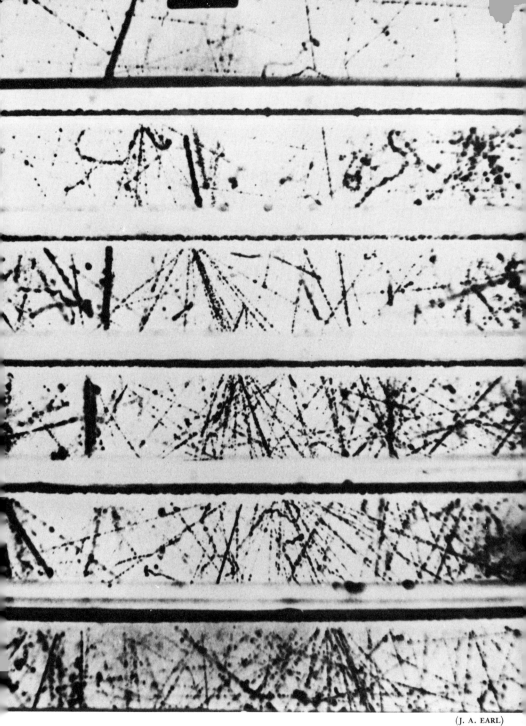

(J. A. EARL)

PUZZLE PICTURE N.   PROBING THE UNKNOWN

What questions can you formulate about this picture of cosmic rays passing through a series of horizontal lead plates in a cloud chamber?

PROBING THE UNKNOWN

You probably accept it as true that matter is made of tiny moving particles, called atoms and molecules, and that these, in turn, are composed of still smaller particles —electrons, protons, and neutrons. You must have wondered how it was possible to discover such tiny, invisible things. How do scientists *know* that electrons revolve around the nuclei of atoms? What makes them so sure that there really are such things as electrons, protons, and neutrons?

It's a long story and a fascinating one that requires a book all its own to relate properly. However, analysis of the photograph on the previous page will provide a glimpse into the kinds of experimental and reasoning processes by which the story was unfolded.

As you may know, the surface of the earth is constantly bombarded from above by vast numbers of nuclear particles and gamma rays (similar to X-rays, but more energetic). The origin of this *radiation* (known as *cosmic rays*) has been found to be enormously energetic nuclear particles that come from outer space. These particles are called *primary* cosmic rays. It has been discovered that most of this original radiation consists of particles called *protons*, with some heavier atomic nuclei accounting for a minor part of the radiation.

As these particles smash into the atmosphere they collide with atoms of oxygen, nitrogen, and the other gases in the air. Large numbers of such atoms are smashed by the collisions into a wide variety of other types of particles, all traveling at high speed. These particles then rain down upon the surface of the earth. In turn, they collide with other atoms and produce still more radiation. This *second-

ary cosmic radiation contains various atomic nuclei, electrons, and gamma rays. The particles lose energy with each collision. Thus the secondary particles have much less energy and penetrating power than the primary ones.

Before 1960 it was not known whether there were any electrons in the primary radiation that came from outer space. An atomic scientist, James A. Earl, decided to set up an experiment to find such primary cosmic ray electrons, if they existed. The way in which he set about solving this problem reveals many interesting facts about scientific method.

By the time the primary cosmic ray particles travel through the hundreds of miles of air, most of them have dissipated their energy by producing cascades of secondary cosmic radiation. So to detect the primary rays it was necessary for Dr. Earl to send his equipment high up into the atmosphere. A balloon was used for this purpose.

Second, he needed some way of detecting the passage of these particles. A "cloud chamber" was selected as the detecting instrument. It is particularly useful for this task because it makes a photographic record of the actual paths of high-speed particles. In this chamber tiny clouds form along such paths very much as vapor trails form behind invisible jet airplanes high in the sky. With the use of the cloud chamber instrument and the permanent record of the observations on film, Dr. Earl could study the paths at leisure long after they occurred. The instrument and the photographic record provided *objective* information that did not depend upon a fleeting, *subjective* impression—the kind a person might receive from the eye.

Third, he needed some way to distinguish between the different kinds of particles. In this case observations of the nature of the tracks on the photograph provide the clues. Electrons are much lighter than protons and most other atomic particles. They are more penetrating and also produce less damage to atoms with which they collide. As a result, electrons produce a light, beaded track on the film, in contrast with the thick, dense track produced by a heavy particle.

Fourth, Dr. Earl needed some way to distinguish between the enormously energetic primary cosmic ray electrons and the less energetic secondary ones. Some idea of the amount of energy possessed by a particle can be obtained from the amount of matter it can penetrate. Lead plates are commonly used for this purpose. Dr. Earl calculated that five lead plates, each a quarter of an inch thick, would be able to stop any of the secondary cosmic ray electrons. Thus any electron that could penetrate so much lead would be identified as a primary particle.

Puzzle Picture N is one of the photographs he took with his equipment in a high-altitude balloon. Six horizontal regions are shown in this picture. Each region contains tracks. The lead plates are the narrow, white, horizontal spaces that separate the sections showing the tracks. The lead plates appear white because the reproduction is a negative, with all dark and light areas reversed.

Study the photograph carefully. Then answer the following questions:

1. What evidence indicates that most of the particles are coming from above?

2. Is there any evidence that some of the particles are relatively slow while others have enormous energies?

3. Which path was probably caused by a primary cosmic ray electron?

4. Find a high-speed secondary cosmic ray electron.

5. Locate the paths of several heavy particles.

6. Gamma rays do not show any tracks in such cloud chamber photographs. But they can be detected by making use of the fact that they frequently cause atomic particles to move. Can you find any such evidence for the existence of gamma rays in this photograph?

Analysis of Puzzle Picture N

1. Each section has more tracks than the one above it, with the greatest number in the lowest section and least in the upper section. This fact indicates that the radiation causing the tracks is coming from above, because high-speed particles produce additional ones by collision with atoms in the air. We would therefore expect to find more tracks at the end of the journey of a very high-speed particle and fewer at the beginning. From these considerations we can infer that most of the particles are coming from above.

2. All objects in motion have *inertia*—the property of continuing in straight-line motion in the same direction. The faster the object (or particle) the greater its inertia and the harder it is to stop or to make it swerve from a straight path. Thus we can get some indication of comparative speeds by the straightness and length of path of a particle. Several straight-line paths that penetrate two or more lead plates are seen in the photograph. The outstanding one is the path along A, B, C, D, E, F, and G (Fig. 22). Place a ruler along the separate sections of the path. They appear to be in a perfectly straight line.

Other straight lines, but shorter, are observed elsewhere in the picture. These are obviously less energetic than the one from A to G.

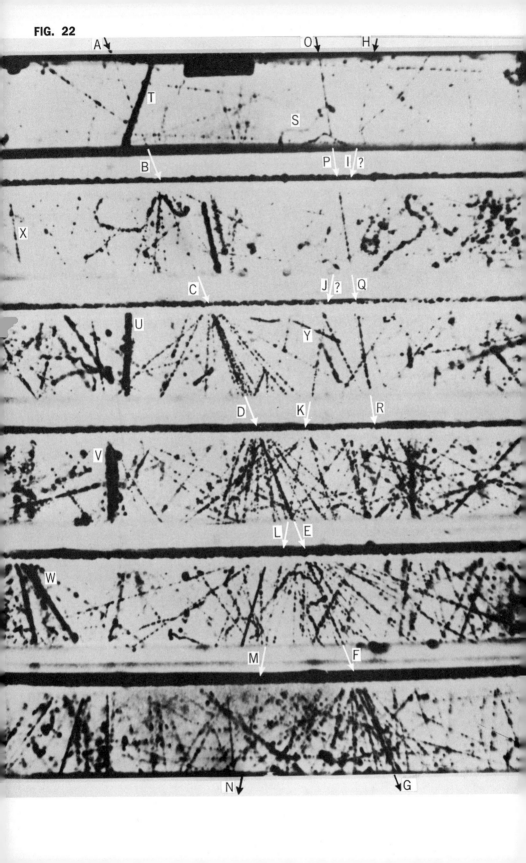

FIG. 22

There are also various zigzag and curly paths. Such paths could not be made by particles with enormous energy, but only by relatively slow ones that are easily deflected by collisions with atoms.

3. It was stated that only the extremely energetic primary cosmic ray electrons could pass through five lead plates. Obviously, the particle that passed from A to G fits this description. The track from O to R penetrates only two plates and is stopped in the third one at R. So it was made by a secondary particle.

But both of the particles are most probably electrons, as noted from the light, beaded tracks and their ability to penetrate lead.

Also observe the way in which the high-speed primary electron produces showers of new secondary particles in each lead plate. Note how new particles radiate outward from the points where the electron hit the plates. This occurs at B, C, D, E, and F. In contrast, observe that this tendency to cause showers of other particles is not as noticeable in the case of the particle that starts at O and ends at R. This is another indication that the particle that produced the path from A to G is far more energetic than the one that passed from O to R.

There seems to be some evidence for another primary particle that passed from H to N. A ruler placed along HN seems to reveal a perfectly straight line. However, it is probably not a primary cosmic ray track for the following reasons. First, primary electrons are quite rare. A large number of photographs must be taken to find one. Thus, the chance that two such particles would appear in one photograph is very small, although it might possibly happen. Therefore, we would be suspicious if we found two such tracks in one picture.

Examining more closely what appears to be a track from H to N, we first observe that it does not seem to produce the type of cascading shower that the particle from A to G produces. Also, the evidence for straight-line motion in the section between I and J is rather flimsy. There are only three small dots in that section that seem to indicate that a particle passed by. It may well be that these three dots just happened to be in a straight line.

Let's look at the section from H to I more closely. Examination of the lower part of the path from H to I shows that the particle seems to veer off to the right. This casts doubt on the hypothesis that it is a primary cosmic ray electron. Perhaps the particle traveling from H toward I collided with an atom and generated two other particles plus an invisible gamma ray that continued straight ahead to generate the three occasional dots in section IJ, and then produced another particle that shot straight ahead from J to N. This would account for the almost straight path from H to N.

However, with our meager knowledge these are merely guesses. An atomic scientist would have greater experience upon which to base an analysis of this particular path.

4. We have already noted a secondary cosmic ray electron along the straight-line path from O to R. Another was noted along the path from J to N. You can find others of this type.

5. Note the very thick, dense tracks at T, U, V, and W. These dense tracks indicate heavy particles. Also note the fact that each of these tracks begins and ends in a lead plate. And in most cases there is evidence that some par-

ticle entering the lead above caused the heavy, dense track below.

6. To find evidence for a gamma ray we should hunt for tracks that start in midair for no apparent reason. Unfortunately we cannot be sure which way the particle making the track was going. It might be suddenly stopped in midair, rather than starting at that point. The evidence for a gamma ray would be clearer if the track were just a completely separate section in midair, with no relationship to other particles or to the lead plates.

Such a track is not so easy to find. However, there is an indication of such a path at X. If you put a ruler across the tops of the points where the other tracks stop at the lead plate above, you will observe that the track at X falls short of touching the lead plate. So the upper part seems to end in midair. So does the lower part. However, we observe that there may be a junction at the bottom of the track with another track off to the left. Is it possible that the track at the left represented a particle that came downward toward the right and then created a particle that shot upward to make track X? We would need more information about tracks to know whether such a sharp change in direction is possible.

Another hypothesis for the formation of this track would be that a gamma ray came in from below, struck an atom, and created two particles that moved upward from the point of collision.

On the basis of the information we have been given, we would have to rate this track as possibly caused by gamma radiation, but it isn't at all certain. An expert would have more information on which to base a judgment.

Another track of this type appears at Y. However, the

evidence is not clear-cut because the track begins and ends too close to other tracks.

This Puzzle Picture illustrates how it is possible to make reasonable judgments in such an abstract area as atomic science. Perhaps you will now have more confidence in your own ability to master advanced branches of scientific research.

PUZZLE PICTURE O.   DISCOVERING HIDDEN PRINCIPLES

A definite set of rules has been followed for the placement of 2 x 2 squares inside larger squares of different sizes. What will our question be?

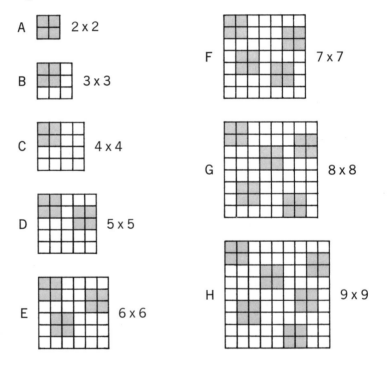

DISCOVERING HIDDEN PRINCIPLES

A basic aspect of scientific method is the search for principles or laws that underlie seemingly disordered events. Such principles or laws reveal basic orderly patterns and thereby provide understanding of and perhaps control over the events.

For example, Newton's Law of Gravitation makes a basic connection between the apparently different events of the falling of an apple and the changing positions of the planets in the sky. When one stops to think of it, it seems rather unlikely that these two very different events would be connected in any way. Yet the same cause operates for both.

The Law of Gravitation enables us to predict what will happen to the speed of an apple and the distance it will move in a given time as it approaches the earth. The law also makes it possible for us to tell where a planet will be in the sky a hundred years from now as it moves around the sun.

The Law of Gravitation also gives us control over this type of event. We can use it to calculate where a cannon shot will hit. And we can use it to send an earth satellite up into the sky, make it orbit around the earth or go around the back of the moon and then return to earth.

For thousands of years it was assumed that all the different creatures on earth were created at the same time and have remained unchanged throughout time. In the past century Darwin's Theory of Evolution connected the development of all living things to each other and showed how the creatures now living could have evolved from others that existed in the past. The ways in which evolution occurred have been shown to follow certain laws and principles which Darwin proposed as part of his theory. These laws and principles enable us to judge what various creatures may have been like in the past and what they might become in the future.

Discovery of such laws and principles is very difficult because they are generally masked by many different kinds of events. It is not easy to pick out the observations that are important in analyzing the events. It is usually necessary to make a great many observations and to hunt for not-so-obvious connections among the different events. As we have seen, we make hypotheses about what the underlying principles might be. We propose such hypotheses for the purpose of pointing out directions for further investigation. Then to investigate the truth or falsity of these hypotheses we devise new experiments and seek additional observations.

This process greatly increases our knowledge even if the hypotheses turn out to be false. Investigations of this kind have frequently produced new information of far greater importance than the original problem would indicate. As an illustration, consider the fact that atomic energy was first observed by Henri Becquerel at the turn of the century while he was looking into the "phosphorescence" (glowing in the dark after exposure to light) of an ore that contained uranium. By accident he discovered that the ore gave off highly penetrating rays of some kind. A few years later the Curies were able to extract radium from the kind of ore Becquerel used in his experiment.

How does one go about discovering underlying principles? How are hypotheses made and checked? We shall illustrate the process by considering the patterns of squares shown in Puzzle Picture O. Certain rules or "laws" were followed in placing the small 2 x 2 squares inside the big ones. We have made your task of discovering the rules easier by placing the large squares in an ordered pattern according to size.

The language of science must be precise, otherwise knowledge of the laws cannot be transmitted to others. Great care is paid to the statement of laws and principles in books so that they are not misused and misinterpreted. Therefore when you think you have mastered the method of placement of squares you are to state the rules so precisely that anyone else could make the same patterns. The purpose of this activity is to provide practice in communicating your ideas to others.

Finally, you are to apply the rules you have discovered to the creation of a pattern for a 12 x 12 square. In effect, this is a prediction which will test the correctness of your rules.

To summarize, your questions are:

1. What are the rules by which the 2 x 2 squares were placed inside the larger squares?

2. State these rules so that another person could repeat the process and arrive at exactly the same patterns.

3. Predict what the pattern for a 12 x 12 square would be like. Make the pattern and then compare it with the one shown in the answer section.

Analysis of Puzzle Picture O

To solve the problem we must search for similarities and differences between the patterns.

Note that the background of each pattern is composed of a gridwork of lines in square formation. We shall refer to each square in this gridwork pattern as "one unit."

Glance down the patterns in sequence, starting with the

2 x 2 square and ending with the 9 x 9 pattern. It is immediately evident that, aside from the 2 x 2 pattern, each has a small 2 x 2 square in the upper left corner. A reasonable hypothesis would be that each pattern starts with the insertion of such a small square.

Now study squares A, B, and C. Observe that there is only one 2 x 2 square in each of these. We also note that there is room for another 2 x 2 square in the 4 x 4, without any overlapping, yet the second small square is not inserted until the 5 x 5 square is reached. Can one of the rules be that 2 x 2 squares may not touch each other? Such a question is really an hypothesis. It immediately suggests a check against the other squares. If this hypothesis is correct, none of the small squares will be found touching each other in any of the patterns.

We find this to be the case. So we may consider that we have probably discovered one of the rules.

What is the rule for placement of the second square? The 5 x 5 square (see Fig. 23) provides a direct clue here because it is the only one with two small squares. We observe that the second square (52) appears one unit below the first square (51). It also appears one unit to the right of the first square. This suggests the hypothesis that the second square in every case is one unit below the first and one unit to the right. We quickly check this hypothesis against the next pattern (6 x 6).

We find that our hypothesis is partly correct. In that pattern the second square (62) is still one unit lower than the first (61), but it is two units to the right of the first one. So that part of our hypothesis which states that the second square is one unit to the right of the first one seems to be wrong.

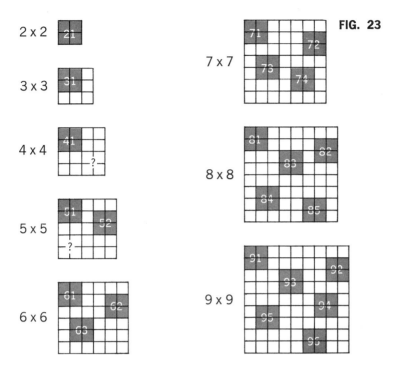

FIG. 23

Actually, we are breaking down these steps into finer divisions than the mind may actually require in a real problem. Many people could check the above hypotheses at a glance. More time is required to explain the idea or to read it than to understand the point by looking at the pattern. Nevertheless it is useful for our understanding of the process to analyze the ideas in such small steps.

Let us now observe how the second 2 x 2 square is placed in the remaining patterns. In the 5 x 5, 6 x 6, and 7 x 7 squares we note that the second squares (52, 62, and 72) are all one unit lower than the first one and that they are always at the right edge. A quick check with the remaining two patterns shows that the same thing applies to them as well. The rule for placement of the second square clearly seems to be that it is at the right edge of the large square and one unit down from the top.

It is not as yet clear what the *general* rule is. The rule for placement of the second square at the right edge of the large one does not seem to help us with regard to placement of the third and fourth squares. There is probably some deeper, underlying rule of which our rule for the second square is but a special case. We will have to find the general rule by examining the patterns more intensively. A good way to proceed is to single out the squares that are likely candidates for third in the sequence of each pattern and see how they are placed.

Let us note that we are assuming in this approach that the sequence of placement is to start at the top and work down one unit at a time. This is still an hypothesis. As we proceed, this must be kept in mind, and we must constantly check with the patterns. If at any point we run into a contradiction, it will be necessary to discard or modify this hypothesis. But if we never find any contradiction, then we shall have strong evidence that the rule is correct as stated.

It should also be noted that this point applies in general to most scientific work. It is really never possible to prove any scientific law or principle absolutely. We test the application of the law again and again, in as many different ways as possible. If we always find that it works, the *evidence* piles up that the law or principle is correct. At a certain point nobody doubts it any more and we consider it to have been *proved*. But the very next experiment, performed differently than before, or more accurately, may turn up a contradiction. That one contradiction forces us to modify our "proven" law in some way.

With regard to our patterns we might assume as an hypothesis that the first square is at the upper left corner and the others follow in sequence, one unit lower than the previous one (if possible). If our hypothesis works for all patterns and enables us to construct them properly, then we could consider it to be proven.

Now let us return to our consideration of the third small square in the sequence. Three small squares do not appear in a large square until the 6 x 6 pattern is reached. We can reasonably assume that we know what the first two squares are and label them 61 and 62. On this basis the remaining one may be labeled 63.

There is a bit of a puzzle with regard to the 5 x 5 square. There seems to be plenty of room for a third square in the lower left-hand corner, as indicated by the question mark. We can put in a 2 x 2 square without violating the rule that it must not touch the others. So there seems to be some other restriction to the placement of another 2 x 2 square in the empty space. We may find a clue by studying the way the third square is placed in the larger patterns.

Observe square 63. It is one unit to the right of 61. But it is also two units below the starting level of the second square. However, we can see that placement of the top of this square one unit below the top of square 62 would have made it touch square 61. It seems reasonable to make the hypothesis that such placement was ruled out by that restriction. This can be quickly checked with the larger patterns. We observe that square 73 is also one unit to the right of 71 and its top two below the top of 72. But a change occurs when we get to 83. The position of 83 seems to suggest that we are permitted to place a square one unit lower than the previous one in the sequence only if it does not touch any other square. Since touching would have occurred in the 5 x 5, 6 x 6, and 7 x 7 patterns, we were apparently forced to go one unit lower.

Also, the placement of the third square in each pattern is always to the right of the first square and never directly underneath. Is it possible that we are not allowed to put a square in the same vertical line as another square? This hypothesis can be quickly checked. No exception is found in any pattern. It therefore seems likely that this is one of the rules for forming the patterns. It also explains why a third square was not permissible in the 5 x 5 pattern.

The difference between the placement of 83 and 93 requires another rule. According to the rules already worked out there is only one possible position for 83. If it were placed one square to either side, it would have touched one of the other squares. However, square 93 has two possible positions. Placement of this square closer to the left rather than to the right suggests that there is some priority with regard to which edge is to be favored.

Many hypotheses are possible at this point, and a number may have to be tried out before one would be found to apply to all. However, by now we have made clear the process of developing the rules and so we can attempt to answer our three questions by stating the rules we have deduced. You may check these with the ones you have formulated. They are:

1. A series of patterns are made inside large squares that have an integral number of units on each edge. These large squares are subdivided into smaller squares one unit on each edge. Squares two units on each edge are then placed inside the larger squares, with their edges always coinciding with the lines formed by the unit squares.

For the purpose of discussion let us refer to the 2 x 2 squares as "small squares." We shall refer to the large squares into which the small ones are placed as "large squares."

2. The small squares are placed inside the large ones in a definite sequence, starting with a first square in the upper left corner of the large square.

3. Small squares may not be directly above or below other small squares.

4. The top of each small square is placed on a line one unit below that of the previous small square provided that no other rules are violated. If it is not possible to place a small square without violation of a rule, then it is placed on the next line that does not result in a violation.

5. Each square is as far as possible laterally from the preceding one. (In other words, if the previous square was at the right side of the large one, the next one is placed as far to the left as possible, and vice versa.)

Check these rules against the patterns in the original figure. Then check its application with the 12 x 12 pattern shown in Fig. 24.

FIG. 24

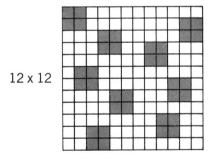

12 x 12

Keep in mind that this may not be the only possible way of stating the rules. It often happens in scientific investigations that different ways of stating laws may lead to the same results. But the different approaches may then suggest new experiments or observations to distinguish between them. Such new experiments often lead to deeper understanding of nature.

Also, we stopped at a 9 x 9 pattern. We could easily devise a 10 x 10 pattern that alters the previous rule in some way and which alters all patterns thereafter. In scientific work, as one delves deeper into more complex areas, it is often found that the laws based upon simple things no longer apply in the same way. It is then necessary to modify the laws and principles so that they reflect the new facts.

It is likely that the deeper we delve into the mysteries of nature the more complex will we find them to be. If that is the case, it is quite likely that continuous modification of our laws and principles will be necessary as science grows and develops.

V / Practice Puzzle Pictures

In Chapter I it was stated that science may be viewed as a general approach to solving problems with "no holds barred." Despite all the specific points that have already been made in this book about scientific method, the list of methods, devices, and tricks that are useful in solving problems is far from exhausted. Each person must learn to wrestle with problems in his own way and to discover how to attack problems in ways best suited to himself.

The key to developing skill in playing the piano is practice. The key to success in lifting weights is to lift a great many weights. The key to mastery of chess is to play chess. And the key to problem-solving ability is to solve a wide variety of problems.

The purpose of the problems in this chapter is to provide additional practice situations dealing with those aspects of scientific method considered up to this point. But they will be of only minor value if you adopt a passive attitude and let the text direct your thinking. You will derive the greatest benefit if you really tackle these problems by yourself. Use the text to test your own ideas or to help you over obstacles that you cannot surmount yourself.

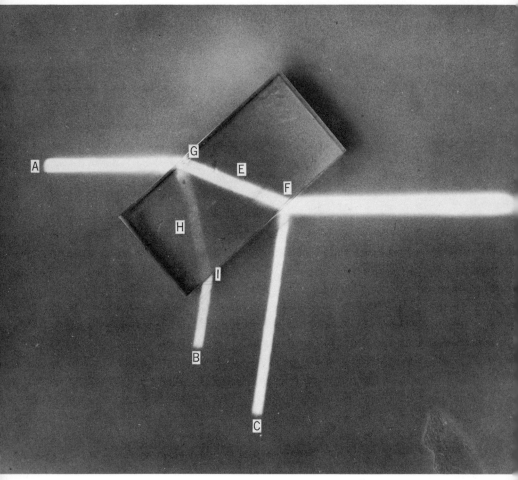

(COURTESY EASTMAN KODAK COMPAN)

PUZZLE PICTURE P.   BEAMS OF LIGHT

This picture shows rays of light entering and leaving the edges
of a rectangular block of glass. What questions occur to you?

BEAMS OF LIGHT

There are four places in Puzzle Picture P where light seems to enter or exit from the glass (ends of the white areas near A, B, C, and D). Only one of these is an entering ray, and the other three are leaving the glass. Our questions are these:

1. Which is the entering ray?
2. Discover the directions of motion of all of the rays.
3. Find six facts about light revealed in this photograph.

After you have completed the answers to these questions, you may wish to pursue additional aspects of this Puzzle Picture. If so, there are additional questions listed after the answers to the three above.

Analysis of Puzzle Picture P

1. The solution to this problem cannot be obtained by logic alone. Certain basic facts must be known, and we can then use these facts to make logical deductions.

One basic fact we need to know is this: Whenever a ray of light strikes a smooth surface, some of it (to a greater or lesser degree) is reflected back from the surface at an equal angle. The nature of this reflection is shown in Fig. 25. It is customary in optics to measure the angles as shown at 1 and 2 in the drawing.

Another basic fact is: The portion of a ray of light that enters a denser transparent material from air bends as shown in Fig. 26. The manner in which it bends as it leaves the denser transparent material (such as glass) is shown in Fig. 27. The light ray continues in the same general direction. Abrupt changes of direction like the one shown in Fig. 28 are not observed.

Let us now examine rays AG, BI, CF, and DF from this

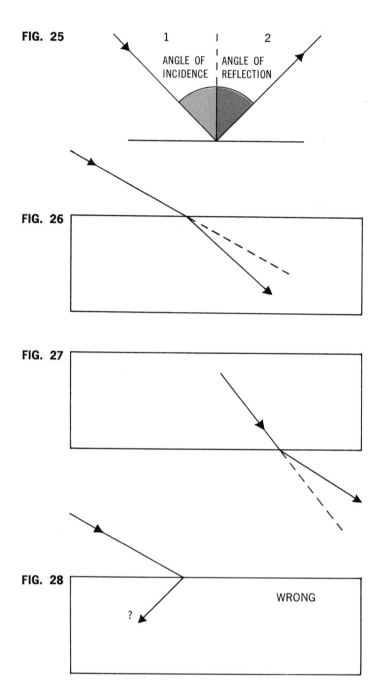

FIG. 25

1   2

ANGLE OF   ANGLE OF
INCIDENCE   REFLECTION

FIG. 26

FIG. 27

FIG. 28

WRONG

?

viewpoint (Fig. 29). One of the rays—CF or DF—might be a
reflected ray because the angles at 1 and 2 are equal, so far as
we can tell. FG and GI inside the glass seem to be a similar
pair of rays undergoing reflection. The general direction of
motion thus seems to be from the area CD toward A.

FIG. 29

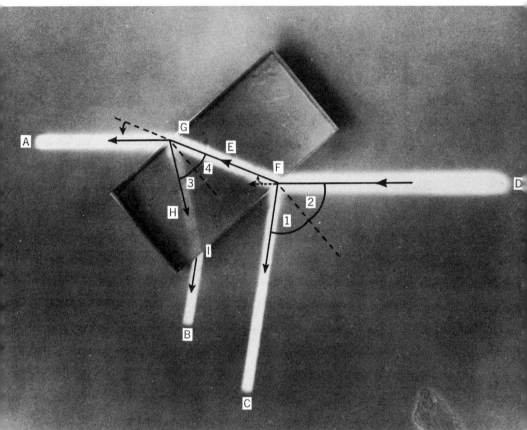

Which ray, CF or DF, is the entering ray? According to
our second rule, ray FG is the continuation of ray DF because they are in the same general direction. An abrupt
change of direction of the kind that would be necessary

if the ray traveled from CF to FG is seen to violate the rule we have stated for motion of rays of light entering a transparent material (see Fig. 28). Thus we can conclude from our observations and rules about light that the entering ray is DF.

2. Ray DF gives rise to a reflected ray (CF) and a portion (FG) that is inside the glass. Ray FG then hits the surface at G and gives rise to a reflected ray (GI) and another ray leaving toward A. Ray BI is clearly a continuation of ray H.

The directions of all the rays have now been deduced, as shown by the arrows in Fig. 29.

3. The following facts about light can be observed in this photograph:

a. All of the beams travel in straight lines in either air or glass.

b. Directions of beams are changed only at boundaries between air and glass surfaces.

c. Part of a light beam (D) that strikes the outside of a block of glass is reflected (C). The angle of reflection equals the angle of incidence. (Angle 1 equals angle 2.)

d. Part of a light beam that strikes the block of glass enters it (E) and is bent (refracted) in such a way that the ray seems to move "more directly" into the glass. (For a more exact formulation look up "refraction" in a physics book.)

e. Part of the light that strikes the surface inside the glass (at G) is reflected in a similar manner to that of the ray striking the glass from outside air. (Angle 3 equals angle 4.)

f. A light ray leaving glass and entering air (Fig. 27) bends slightly. The direction of bending is such that it shifts "closer" to the glass. (Again, for a more detailed discussion of refraction, consult a physics book.)

Now try your skill with the following additional questions:

4. How can we explain the extra width of beam DF?

5. Why do the rays all seem to have abrupt beginnings and endings?

6. Why does one of the rays inside the glass appear much dimmer than the others?

7. Was this picture taken only by the light from the beams, or was another source of light used?

8. How do you explain the bright lines along portions of the edge of the glass block?

9. On the long side of the block at G you see both the top and bottom edges of the block. But the bottom edge is not visible in the long side of the block at FI. Why?

10. Why does the glass block cast shadows along the narrow edges? Why is the shadow more marked at the lower left?

Answers to Questions 4–10:

4. The beam is probably formed by a convex lens (A in Fig. 30) that causes a beam of light to converge and thereby to become narrower as it proceeds.

5. The projector (P in Fig. 31) is probably tilted downward slightly. The beam becomes visible by upward reflection where the lower part of the beam first touches the surface (at D). The upper part of the beam continues downward at a very slight angle and reaches the surface (probably white paper) at points A and B.

6. The following explanation of why beam H is much dimmer than the others is offered without any certainty that it is correct. However, it is reasonable, based on the facts and principles of light, and may be considered to be

FIG. 30

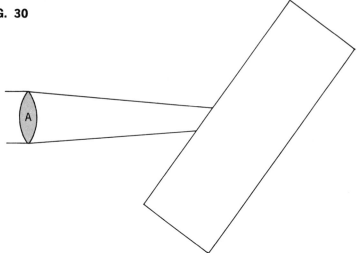

a kind of "theory" which is subject to further experimentation and checking.

Some of the rays of light from the projector probably go over the edge of the glass and strike the top, as happens to ray 1 in Fig. 31. Such a ray would be refracted down-

FIG. 31

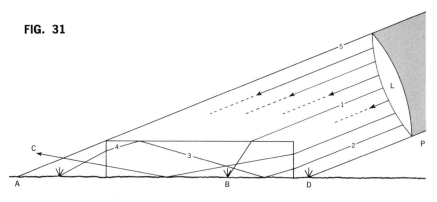

ward and exit at the bottom of the glass at B. Then it would hit the white surface below and bounce up in a diffuse manner, reach the eye and thereby reveal the place where it struck the surface. Thus, the path for this portion would become visible.

Those rays from the projector that enter the side of the glass (as exemplified by ray 2) would be at such a glancing angle that they could not escape from the glass at that point. They would undergo a regular reflection (mirror-like), as shown by ray 3, and then be reflected again to the top to produce ray 4 that can exit from the narrow side of the glass toward A.

The path of the light would be revealed mainly by the rays that enter the glass from the top rather than by those that enter it from the side.

If ray 5 is the uppermost ray in the original beam, we should see a sharp cut-off on the white surface where that beam reaches it.

The photographer who made the picture probably adjusted the angles so that all of the path was visible. If he were concerned with revealing the reflected beam (H in Fig. 29), additional adjustments could probably have been made to extend the cut-off point still further.

Of course not all rays take the paths shown in Fig. 31. There may be several ways for rays to get to a particular point. Thus we do see some light along the path H, even though dimmer than that produced by the other rays.

7. The dark shadows and gray appearance of the background indicate that a dim supplementary source was used from a direction at lower left.

8. The edge of the glass is probably ground to prevent scratching of the fingers when it is handled. If so, this small, rough edge reflects light diffusely to become more visible. (Consult a physics book.) Note that these bright lines appear mainly near the places where the light beam enters or leaves the glass.

9. The camera was pointing down toward the glass plate. It is centered directly over the edge at FI. As a result, both

the top and bottom edges of the plate are in the same line with the lens of the camera, and so both appear as one line.

On the other hand, the remaining long edge is off center, and both top and bottom edges can then be seen.

10. Fig. 32 shows how light rays travel from the supplementary light used to illuminate the background. Rays 1, 2, 3, 4, and 5 bend closer to the glass as they enter and therefore are made to spread out more as they hit the bottom of the glass at A. The region at A is then only moderately illuminated.

FIG. 32

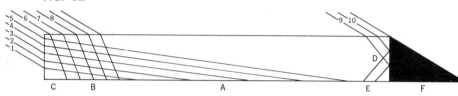

Rays 6, 7, 8, etc., bend as shown to add illumination at B, but not at C. Thus region B which receives light from two directions is brighter than region C, which then appears as a kind of darker area or shadow, but not completely dark.

Rays 9 and 10 enter and bend as shown, but then strike the edge (D) at such an angle that they cannot get out at D. They are reflected toward E. Region E therefore gets additional light (which you can verify from the photograph, while region F gets none and is a dark shadow).

Study the original photograph and note how the dark and light regions correspond to the predictions made above. If you knew a great deal more about light, it would be possible to make further deductions about the directions of the light rays and the dimensions of the block from the distribution of the light and dark areas.

PUZZLE PICTURE Q.   TELESCOPE MIRROR

This Puzzle Picture shows the back of the glass mirror for the world's largest telescope, stationed at Mount Palomar in California. What questions can you formulate about this photograph?

TELESCOPE MIRROR

Here are some of the questions that might be asked about Puzzle Picture Q:

1. What is the geometrical pattern of the mirror?
2. Why was this pattern used?
3. What is the approximate diameter of the disk?
4. What is the man on the left doing?
5. What was the approximate height above the floor of the camera that took the picture?
6. Is the back of the mirror (side toward the camera) flat or curved?
7. What kind of lighting was used to take the picture?

Analysis of Puzzle Picture Q

1. The easiest way to determine the basic pattern is to place a thin sheet of paper over the photograph and to trace it with a pencil. To simplify the figure, locate the centers of each of the circular holes in the glass by pressing very lightly with a pencil and connect the points with lines. Such a tracing is shown in Fig. 33.

Using a ruler, we observe that the centers of the holes all fall on intersecting straight lines. Although the upper left portion of the disk is lost in darkness, it is possible to locate the circular edge by drawing continuations of these lines. We are aided by the probable assumption that the mirror is circular and that the number of triangular sections are equal on each side of the center of the mirror.

Points A, B, and C are seen to lie on the circle. It is therefore reasonable to connect A, B, and C to form a triangle. Extend lines CD and AE. They meet at F. The symmetry suggests that this point is on the edge of the disk. Points A, C, and F seem to form a large equilateral triangle. If we

FIG. 33

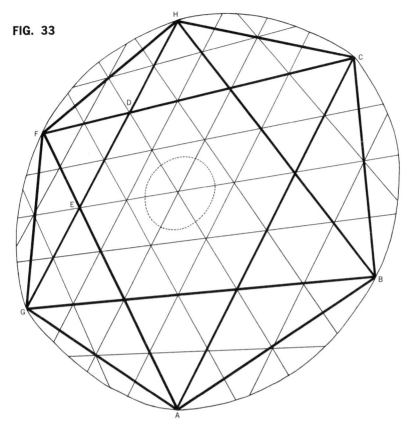

designate the distance between holes as d, the length of a side of this large equilateral triangle is $6d$.

There is another triangle of the same kind (BGH). Points A, B, C, H, F, and G are seen to form a hexagon, enclosed in the circle. It is probable that the hexagon is regular (equal-sided and equal-angled) but that this fact is masked by distortions in the photograph due to perspective.

We can now draw the complete pattern without the distorting effect of perspective, as shown in Fig. 34. Select a unit, such as one inch, for the distance d. Draw an equilateral triangle (ABC) 6 units on each side. Mark off the 6 units on each edge—as shown on each side of triangle

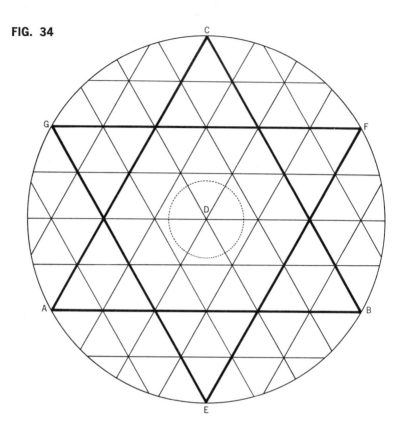

FIG. 34

ABC. Then connect all points lying on lines parallel to the sides. It is then easy to locate the center of the circle at D and the interlocking triangle EFG.

2. A solid block of glass would be extremely heavy. The weight was substantially reduced by molding straight ribs of glass across the back. The glass must have a substantial thickness to maintain its shape, an extremely important factor in a large telescope where great accuracy of surface shape is required. A thin mirror would bend more, especially for so large a weight of glass. This would alter reflections from the mirror and distort the image.

Circular holes at the intersections of the triangle are

142

probably used to reduce weight, and at the same time to reduce strains in the glass as it cools from the molten state.

Triangular structures have more rigidity than any other shapes. It is also reasonable to suppose that the triangles are equilateral. Assuming this, we see that the general structure follows quite logically from the properties of the glass and its intended use.

3. Measure the height of the man at the right with a ruler. It is 6.6 cm. on the drawing. The vertical radius of the disk, measured slightly to the left of the man, is close to 8 cm. The diameter would therefore be about 16 cm. The man is probably close to 6 feet tall. With this assumption we can estimate the diameter of the disk as follows:

$$\frac{D}{6 \text{ ft.}} = \frac{16 \text{ cm.}}{6.6 \text{ cm.}}$$

$$D = 14.6 \text{ ft.}$$

Converting this to inches, we obtain:

$$D = 12 \times 14.6 \text{ ft.}$$

$$= 175 \text{ in. (approximately)}$$

Since the man is a bit closer to the camera than the disk, he should appear relatively larger on the photograph. We can therefore consider the estimate of 175 inches as probably on the low side. (Actually, this mirror has a diameter of 200 inches. So we see that our estimate is reasonably close.)

4. We note a very bright area between the men, centering on one of the holes. We also note a wire along the floor at bottom right and going up to the man's hand. It is probable that an electric light has been placed in one of the holes. The man is seen peering down into one of the

sections of glass, apparently looking through the glass at the light.

The circumstances strongly imply that he is examining the glass for imperfections.

5. The planks of wood on which the disk rests seem to be parallel to each other. Place a thin sheet of paper on the photograph and trace several points on the lines of these planks. Also trace the outline of the man as shown in Fig. 35. Continue all the lines drawn from the planks. They seem to meet approximately in a region around A. Draw horizontal line AB. This line is on the same level as the camera. It cuts across the man's legs just above the knees. Thus the camera was held rather low—probably about two feet above the floor. This is further verified, at least approximately, by the way the upper part of the disk is reduced in apparent size because of extra distance from the camera.

FIG. 35

We also note that we can see the lower parts of all horizontal lines of glass, including the lowest line. It appears that the disk is standing vertically on its edge. Since we can see the bottom of the lowest line of glass, we can infer that the camera was even lower than that line.

The slight difference between the line AB in Fig. 35 and the lowest line of glass is probably due to placement of the planks only approximately parallel to each other, and not exactly so.

6. The lines drawn on the tracing (Fig. 33) are all straight. From this fact we can infer that the back is straight and not curved.

7. The shadows in the holes indicate a strong light at the lower right of the photograph. The shadow of the electric line on the glass and shadow of the man on the right indicate the presence of another light off to the left. This is further confirmed by the bright area on the floor at lower left.

The dark area at the upper left of the disk is probably due to the extra distance of that part from the lamp at the right. It is likely that the light at the left is a spotlight that is illuminating only a portion of the disk, leaving the upper left in darkness.

We also observe evidence of lights behind the glass disk at four or five places where there are local bright spots. These lights were probably used to increase the dramatic effect of the picture.

PUZZLE PICTURE R.   NIGHT PHOTOGRAPH

This photograph is a time exposure of an observatory dome at night. The streaks above the dome are the apparent paths of stars formed as the earth rotated. There should be plenty of inspiration for questions in this scene.

(COURTESY OF DALE P. CRUIKSHANK AND SKY PUBLISHING CO

NIGHT PHOTOGRAPH

Here are the questions for Puzzle Picture R. No doubt you have formulated others that are not on this list:

1. What details about the way the photograph was taken can be inferred from this Puzzle Picture?

2. Is the North Star located exactly at true north?

3. For how long a time was the film exposed?

4. What caused the straight streak in the sky at left center, in contrast to the circular streaks everywhere else?

5. What may have caused the zigzag streak near the bottom of the picture?

6. Was the observatory dome moved while the photograph was being taken?

7. Is there any general illumination from the night sky?

8. The brightest streak of a star seems to be the one nearest the center of the arcs. Was it necessarily caused by the brightest star?

9. How would you reconstruct the relative positions of the stars from this photograph?

Analysis of Puzzle Picture R

1. We observe that the streaks of the stars are circular arcs centering around a point in the upper right-hand portion of the photograph. Such streaks would occur if the camera lens was left open for a few hours. As the earth rotates on its axis all the stars seem to rotate around the point in the sky toward which the axis points. This center of all the star streaks is exactly north. Since we observe this point to be in the picture, the camera must have been pointing north at the time the photograph was taken.

It would seem from the picture that the camera was pointed, not exactly north, but a bit to the west (left) of it.

However, this conclusion would not necessarily be correct if what we see is an enlargement of a small portion of the actual negative.

Since exposure to bright light for several hours would probably have completely fogged the film, it can be inferred that the lights in the observatory were not on all the time—perhaps for only a few minutes.

2. The North Star is used by navigators to locate north because it appears close to the spot in the sky where the earth's axis points. If it were exactly at that point, then we should observe a very bright spot in the photograph exactly at the center of the arcs.

There is no such spot in the picture, but there is a very bright streak above the center and close by. In all probability this streak was caused by the North Star, which is the brightest star in that region of the sky.

An astronomer could use this photograph to determine the exact location of the North Star in relation to true north.

3. We can get a close estimate of the exposure time of the film by measuring the angles that are formed by the arcs in relation to the estimated center. Fig. 36 shows a tracing of three such angles, based upon the star streaks AB, CD, and EF. They all measure within a degree of 56°. We would expect them to be exactly equal from the fact that all stars seem to rotate once in 24 hours. The differences are undoubtedly due to slight inaccuracy in locating the center of the arcs.

If we compare the measured angle of "rotation" of the sky to 360° (the full circle), we can find the fraction of a day occupied in taking the picture. The angle is measured to be 56°, on the average. Thus, $\dfrac{56}{360}$ of a day was the time

FIG. 36

of the exposure. This is $\dfrac{56}{360} \times 24$ hours, or 3.74 hours, or about 3 hours and 44 minutes.

How accurate is this estimate? We note that the three angles were measured to be within $1°$ of each other. An angle of $1°$ represents $\dfrac{1}{360}$ of a rotation, or $\dfrac{1}{360}$ of 24 hours, or 4 minutes. So our estimate is probably accurate to within that period of time. Note how easy it is to achieve a surprising degree of accuracy by simple methods based upon sound reasoning.

4. The straight streak at left center was obviously not caused by a star, or it would have been curved. Yet it seems to have been an object in the sky.

A bright meteor could have caused such a straight streak as it moved across the sky and disappeared in a few seconds.

It is interesting to note the varying brightness of the line. This indicates that the meteor changed in brightness as it moved. If we knew the direction from which the meteor came, we could make inferences about the "life history" of the meteor during its brief flash through the sky.

5. The zigzag streak at the bottom could have been caused by a moving light—perhaps a flashlight carried by a person walking about the grounds.

6. The vague dark areas above the dome indicate that it moved during the time the film was exposed. The projecting structure at the top of the dome would then have covered different parts of the sky for different times to cause some of the star streaks to be reduced in brightness.

We observe that the streaks are just barely reduced in brightness at the extreme left. The projection of the dome was therefore in this position a relatively short time. But some of the streaks just left of the projection and also at the right of the center of the dome are much dimmer. These must have been areas where the dome remained for a substantial part of the exposure.

The very short star streaks to the right of center just above the dome are interesting. They could have been caused by the shape of the projection (a slot in the dome) through which the telescope points up at objects in the sky. The short streaks might represent the portion of time during which the star moved across the slot as it faced toward the camera.

7. The general background of the sky is a dark gray, not an absolute black. We observe a black area at the right of the top of the dome where the projecting slot was in the way. Obviously some small illumination does come from the sky in general.

8. The closer a star is to the center of rotation the shorter will its arc be. As a result it moves more slowly on the film and has more time to record its image. Thus we would expect the stars closest to the center of rotation to give the brightest tracks. It could well be that a star farther from the center and with a dimmer track is actually brighter.

We might make some inferences about relative brightness by measuring the brightness of the track in relation to its distance from the center of rotation.

Of course if we observe one star to have a brighter track than another that is closer to the center, then we can be quite sure that the star with the brighter track is really brighter.

9. We could obtain the relative positions of the stars from the locations of the starting or ending points of the streaks (except for those blocked by the projection).

VI / Measurement and Mathematics

There have now been a number of instances in which we were required to measure certain features in a Puzzle Picture in order to solve a problem. Then some simple kind of calculation had to be performed to obtain the answer to a question.

In this chapter we shall investigate this aspect of scientific method more fully with a series of problems designed to show how measurement and mathematics are used as tools. They are powerful tools and valuable not only in science but in every walk of life.

Of course we are limited in what we can do with photographs as sources for problems, and also by the possible limitations of the reader's mathematical knowledge. But we must assume at least some knowledge of practical geometry.

We also recommend the use of a ruler marked off in centimeters and tenths of a centimeter (millimeters). The use of this metric unit and decimal fractions rather than the ⅛ths and ¹⁄₁₆ths of the customary inch measurements will make calculations much easier. (You may find that your measurements will differ slightly from those given in the text because of distortions resulting from the printing process.)

(LICK OBSERVATORY PHOTOGRAPH)

PUZZLE PICTURE S.   MEASURING THE MOON'S MOUNTAINS

Another picture of the moon? What can we be after this time?
Take a look at the shadows. Some are long; others are short. What
questions does this fact suggest?

MEASURING THE MOON'S MOUNTAINS

The power of mathematical reasoning in scientific work may be illustrated by the way in which it is used to obtain information about the moon, sun, stars, and other objects in the sky. After all, we learn about these objects far out in space only by means of the small amount of light that they send us. Yet we know a really amazing number of facts about them. Consider one example of how we obtain such information.

Puzzle Picture S shows a portion of the moon when we see exactly half of it illuminated by the sun. The questions you are to attempt to answer are:

1. What is the approximate diameter of the large crater to the left of D? (Assume that the diameter of the moon is 2,160 miles.)

2. What is the height of the rim of this crater above the relatively flat area in the center?

To increase the accuracy of measurement of the small distances involved, a 10X enlargement of the crater is shown in the inset. Measure the distances of the enlargement with a ruler and then divide by 10 to obtain the equivalent distance on the main photograph.

We have also made your task easier by drawing certain basic reference lines on the picture. Line AB divides the moon into its equal dark and light halves at this particular phase. Point C locates the center of the visible disk of the moon.

Analysis of Puzzle Picture S

1. Approximate measurement of the diameter of the crater is relatively easy. We simply measure the diameter of the crater on the photograph and compare it with the

known radius of the moon. For our purposes it will be sufficiently accurate to assume that the radius of the moon is 1,080 miles.

Let us note that there are certain assumptions that we must keep in mind. There is some distortion in dimensions as one proceeds away from the center of the picture toward the outer edge of the disk of the moon. This distortion is due to the fact that a spherical object is being represented on a flat surface. To reduce this error and keep it within bounds for our very approximate calculations we have selected a crater that is rather close to the center. Should you wish to make more accurate calculations corrections would have to be made for this distortion. You may then also want to use a more accurate value of the moon's diameter.

Use a ruler to measure the line AB (the diameter) in the picture. It is 17.3 centimeters. Thus 17.3 centimeters represents 2,160 miles. One centimeter (cm.) represents $\frac{1}{17.3}$ of 2,160 miles, or about 125 miles. In effect, you are considering the photograph as a map and using a proportioned scale to convert distances on the map to actual distances.

Now measure the diameter of the crater at D. From the inset we find it to be 2.9 cm. Divide by 10 to obtain the equivalent distance on the main photograph. We obtain a distance of 0.29 cm. for the diameter of the crater. The actual diameter, therefore, is 0.29 × 125, or 36.2 miles.

2. We will approach the problem of estimating the height of the rim by making a drawing to help us analyze the situation.

In Fig. 37 the horizontal lines at the right represent parallel rays coming from the sun. Line AB represents the boundary between the illuminated and dark areas when

FIG. 37

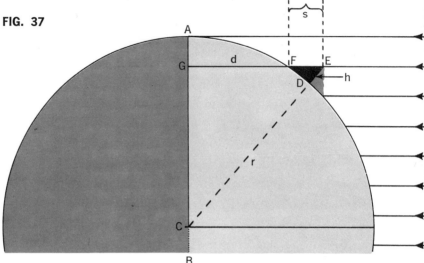

exactly half the moon appears dark, as is the case in this Puzzle Picture. C is the center of the moon.

ED represents a mountain that casts a shadow that extends to F. The length of the shadow, as seen from the earth, is EF (from the mountaintop to the edge of the shadow).

Draw EG perpendicular to AB. This is the observed distance of the mountaintop from the shadow line (AB).

Both EF (the length of the shadow as seen from the earth) and EG (distance of the mountaintop from the line of darkness) are measurable in the photograph.

A bit of geometry is now needed to obtain a relationship between these quantities. Triangles EDF and CEG are right triangles. Also, angle FED is the same as angle CEG. So triangles EDF and CEG are similar, and we can now state the following proportion:

$$\frac{EG}{EC} = \frac{ED}{EF}$$

EG is the perpendicular distance from the mountaintop

156

to the shadow line that divides the moon in half. Let us call this distance d.

EC is the radius of the moon plus the height of the mountain. Since the few miles height of the mountain is very small compared with the thousand-mile radius of the moon, we can consider EC to be very nearly equal to the radius, for practical purposes. Let us call the radius r.

ED is the height of the mountain. Call this h.

EF is the observed length of the shadow. Call this s.

Substituting the shorter symbols d, r, h, and s, the proportion becomes:

$$\frac{d}{r} = \frac{h}{s} \text{ or } h = \frac{d}{r} \times s$$

The ratio $\frac{d}{r}$ is easily obtained by comparing d and r as they appear in the photograph. Since we are interested only in a ratio, it does not matter whether we measure the distances in miles, inches, centimeters, or any other units. Also, we may measure the dimensions in the 10X enlargement and obtain more accurate values.

We find d to be 2.55 cm. and r to be 8.65 cm. Thus:

$$h = \frac{d}{r} \times s = \frac{2.55s}{8.65} = .295s$$

The height of the mountain is .295 times the observed length of the shadow.

Now we need to know the length of the shadow. We can use the method of measuring distances explained in question 1. You will recall that a measured distance of 1 cm. on the photograph equals 125 miles. Measure the length of the shadow on the magnified inset and divide by 10. We obtain for s a value of .09 cm. This represents .09 × 125, or 11.25 miles. Since $h = .295s$, the height of the crater is .295 × 11.25 miles, or 3.3 miles.

That was not too complicated. Now proceed on your own and measure the diameters and heights of a few more craters and other features of the moon.

PUZZLE PICTURE T. A PROBLEM IN PERSPECTIVE

Since this Puzzle Picture appears in a section devoted to measurement, it is clear what direction your questions might take.

A PROBLEM IN PERSPECTIVE

We continue our discussion of the use of mathematics and measurement in scientific method with some interesting problems involving perspective. In Puzzle Picture T we observe a long walk covered with a roof supported by poles. Note that there are three groups of people in the picture.

Answer the following questions:

1. Is the walk straight?
2. Is it level?
3. What is the height of a pole?
4. What is its diameter?
5. What is the width of the walk (between centers of poles)?
6. How high off the ground was the camera that took the picture?
7. What inference can be made about the camera from the answer to question 6?
8. Note the line across the walk between the first set of poles that are visible. Can you calculate from the dimensions in this photograph the camera's distance from this first line? Perhaps you will be able to compute the actual distances between poles along the walk.

We might add that some of these are rather difficult questions and will require careful analysis on your part. Although it is possible to obtain some relationships between the dimensions of the walk, we did not succeed in computing exact distances (see the analysis section which follows). But it may be possible to do so. We leave this question as a challenge to those with a high degree of mathematical ability.

Analysis of Puzzle Picture T

1. The key to the answer to question 1 is the fact that straight lines in the real world are photographed in most cameras as straight lines. We say "most" because special "wide-angle" lenses can distort straight lines noticeably and make them appear curved. But for ordinary cameras with reasonably good lenses actual straight lines photograph as straight lines.

Also, if we see a straight line on the photograph we can be reasonably certain (but not absolutely so) that the real line was straight.

To find out if the walk is straight, place a ruler on the similar points on the photograph of the walk, as shown by the lines starting at A, B, C, D, and E in Fig. 38. All are quite straight and meet at a point (F). So we can reasonably conclude that the walk is straight.

FIG. 38

2. The puddles of water on the walk don't seem to be flowing away. So we may infer that the walk is rather level.

3. To obtain an estimate of the height of a pole we need to compare it to some object whose height we know. The two women at the right provide a clue. They seem to be of normal proportions and average height. Wearing low heels, they would probably be about 5 feet 4 inches tall.

We cannot compare the lengths of their images on the photograph with that of the poles directly since the women are at a different distance from the camera than the first pole. However, we can make a comparison by taking into account the principles of perspective. Let us consider some of these principles.

If the tops and bottoms of the poles are connected with lines, as shown in the tracing (Fig. 39), we obtain a series of smaller and smaller rectangles. The poles seem to come

FIG. 39

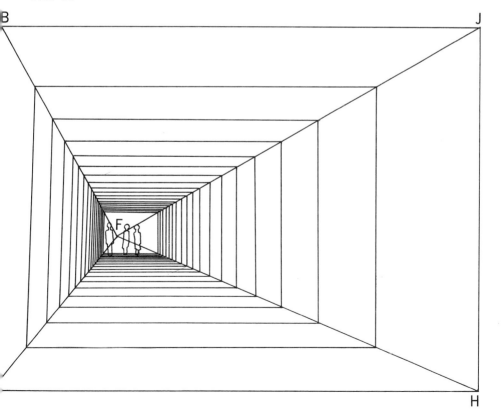

closer and closer together with increasing distance. At a very great distance the poles will appear to be very tiny and will shrink to almost nothing. This is the "vanishing point" (F).

In the photograph all lines actually parallel to lines AF, BF, CF, DF, and EF will appear to converge at F. In the actual scene of which this photograph was made, if we looked at point F our line of sight would be parallel to the lines connecting similar points on the poles.

The height of the woman who is closest to the camera can be compared with the height of a pole by drawing line FG (Fig. 38) from the top of her head (G) to the vanishing point (F). It happens that she is standing on the line connecting the bottoms of the poles (EF). So line FG projects her height on the pole at HI. In effect she would appear to be as high as the length of HI if she were standing at pole H.

Measure the height of the pole (HJ) on the photograph. It is 8.4 cm. Measure the projected height of the woman (HI). It is 5.5 cm. We estimate her height to be 5 ft. 4 in., or 5⅓ ft., or 5.33 ft. We can now make this proportion:

$$\frac{\text{Height of pole}}{\text{Height of woman}} = \frac{\text{Height of pole on picture}}{\text{Height of woman on picture}}$$

$$\frac{h}{5.33 \text{ ft.}} = \frac{8.4 \text{ cm.}}{5.5 \text{ cm.}}$$

$$h = \frac{5.33 \times 8.4}{5.5}$$

$$= 8.14 \text{ ft.}$$

$$= 8 \text{ ft. approx.}$$

Of course the result is not too exact because of our assumption that an "average" height for a woman is 5 feet 4 inches. It would be helpful to use some other object for an independent estimate, but we do not seem able to find one in the picture. So we shall have to consider our estimate as a rough approximation.

4. It is interesting first to estimate the diameter of the pole by eye, then make a more accurate estimate by the following method:

The width of the pole on the photograph measures .42 cm. What does this represent in terms of the actual width of the pole? From the previous answer we note that the pole's height of 8.14 ft. is represented by a measurement on the photograph of 8.4 cm. Think of the photograph as a map drawn to scale. In that case if 8.4 cm. represents 8.14 ft., then 1 cm. represents $\frac{8.14}{8.4}$ of 1 ft., or $\frac{8.14}{8.4} \times 12$ in., or 11.6 in. A measurement of .42 cm. on the photograph therefore means .42 $\times$ 11.6 in., or 4.9 in. Thus the pole has a diameter of about 5 in.

5. The pole at HJ (Fig. 38) and the width of the walk at AH are approximately (but not exactly) equally distant from the camera. We can compare the lengths HJ and AH to obtain an approximation of the width of the walk.

Measure with a ruler the distance across the walk from the right side of the first pole on the right to the right side of the first pole on the left. We find it to be 11.8 cm. We know that 1 cm. on the pole represents an actual distance of 11.6 in. So 11.8 cm. represents 11.8 $\times$ 11.6 in., or 137 in. Convert this to feet by dividing by 12. We obtain a width of 11.4 ft.

6. In Fig. 38 we observe that the line of the tops of the poles (FD) slants downward toward F. That is because the line of the tops of the poles is above the camera. On the other hand, the line of the bottoms of the poles (EF) slants

upward toward F. That is because the bottoms of the poles are below camera level.

Where is the line on the poles that connects all the points at the same level as the camera? It is obviously a line that does not slant up or down. This line can be located in relation to the vertical poles by drawing a perpendicular (FK) from F to the pole (HJ). The height of the camera above the ground is then the same as the height of K on the pole.

Measure HK on the photograph and compare with HJ. We measure it to be 3.4 cm. This distance represents $3.4 \times$ 11.6 in., or 39.4 in., or $\dfrac{39.4 \text{ in.}}{12}$, or 3.4 ft. Therefore the camera was about 3.3 ft. off the ground. Note the way the horizontal line FK cuts across approximately the same points on the bodies of the two groups of people in the distance and the women close to the camera. This fact confirms our estimate of camera height and also strengthens our previous conclusion that the walk is straight and level.

7. If the photographer used a camera with a direct viewer he would have had to stoop or kneel to the 3.3-ft. level to get the picture. This is possible, but not too common a practice.

The fact that the camera was held 3.3 ft. from the ground indicates that it is probably the kind suspended from a strap around the neck, with the photographer looking down into a viewer at the top of the camera.

8. We can obtain a partial answer to this question from the fact that an object twice as far from the camera will appear half as tall. Of course the objects should be in approximately the same line or an error is introduced because of the difference in angle. This error will not be too large for our purposes if we compare the heights of the various

poles in Fig. 38. The poles on the left are more in line with the camera than those on the right and are therefore better for our purpose.

The height of the nearest pole on the left is 8.8 cm. The second pole is 6.2 cm.; the third, 4.8 cm.; the fourth, 3.9 cm. Somewhere between the third and fourth poles there would be one with an image in the photograph half the size of the first pole. Such a pole would be 4.4 cm. high (half of 8.8). This is just about midway between 4.8 cm. (the height of pole 3) and 3.9 cm. (the height of pole 4). If we call the distance between poles d, we might say that the pole that produces an image half the size of the first pole is estimated to be very approximately 2.5d farther than the first pole seen in the photograph.

If the "half-size" pole is 2.3d beyond the first and is also twice as far from the camera, this must mean that the first pole is 2.5d from the camera (Fig. 40). This locates the

FIG. 40

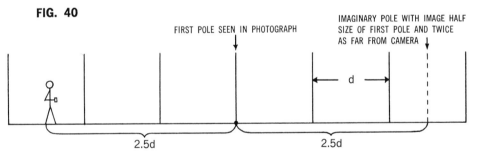

FIRST POLE SEEN IN PHOTOGRAPH

IMAGINARY POLE WITH IMAGE HALF SIZE OF FIRST POLE AND TWICE AS FAR FROM CAMERA

d

2.5d   2.5d

camera in relation to the poles although it does not give us an absolute distance in feet. Such a calculation is beyond the scope of this book and we are not sure that it can be done. However, for those with mathematical ability and some knowledge of geometry and algebra it would be interesting to attempt such a calculation, based on the dimensions observed in the photograph.

PUZZLE PICTURE U.   MEASUREMENTS AND LOGICAL REASONING

We encountered an enlargement of this scene in Puzzle Picture I. You will recall that this structure is a radome in Massachusetts which houses radar equipment. Now see if you can formulate various questions, with emphasis upon measurement and calculation.

MEASUREMENTS AND LOGICAL REASONING

Answer these questions about Puzzle Picture U:

1. What inferences can you make about the materials and method of construction of the radome?

2. What is the diameter of the sphere?

3. What are the approximate lengths of the straight pieces connecting points around the sphere?

4. Throughout most of the radome's surface the straight lines on the sphere appear dark. But slightly above the center of the picture of the sphere they become much whiter. Why?

5. Is the material of the sphere perfectly white?

6. How far away from the sphere was the cameraman?

7. How long is the boom on the crane?

Analysis of Puzzle Picture U

1. Note that there seem to be numerous wrinkles in the spherical surface. These lead us to believe that it is composed of a clothlike material.

Although the short, straight pieces all around the sphere appear to be rigid, it is possible that they are made of a stretchy material like rubber that is pulled straight. They might also be made of a material like cloth or rope. We might doubt the use of metal because radar waves tend to be stopped by a metal frame. And the radar waves must get through the sphere in order to detect distant objects. But perhaps the short radar waves could get through an open metal network.

How is such a structure supported? There are several possibilities. One simple method would be to use air pressure to blow it up like a balloon. Such a structure would require no internal support and would therefore be ex-

167

tremely light. The straight ropes, or whatever they are, would then act as a support to keep the "balloon" spherical and to prevent it from moving about in the wind. Of course it is quite possible that additional strength could be given by some kind of internal bracing.

2. The men standing at the top of the radome enable us to estimate the diameter of the sphere. Use a ruler and magnifying glass to measure their heights on the picture. (The large photograph, Puzzle Picture I, page 74, is better for this purpose.) Allow for the bottom of the legs, which are hidden by a portion of the sphere. The heights of the men are about .4 cm. on the picture. The diameter of the sphere at the widest point is 13.4 cm. (There seems to be a slight reduction in diameter in a vertical direction—perhaps because of the weight of the structure.) Assuming a height of 6 ft. for the men, the diameter of the sphere seems to be: $\frac{13.4}{.4} \times 6$ ft., or 201 ft., or approximately 200 ft.

3. The shortest length of the straight supports at the middle of the photograph (Puzzle Picture I) measures about .9 cm. long, while the longest is about 1.4 cm.

The men on top measure .4 cm. and are about 6 ft. tall. Thus 1 cm. represents $\frac{6}{.4}$, or 15 ft. On this scale the short lengths are .9 $\times$ 15, or 13.5 ft. long, and the long ones are 1.4 $\times$ 15, or 21 ft. long. (We shall see later that the camera was quite far from the sphere, and the error introduced by assuming the straight supports to be at about the same distance as the men is quite small and can be ignored in our rough estimates.)

4. If the straight lengths are covered with a smooth, glossy surface, then to some extent they will tend to reflect

light as a mirror. In such reflection the angle of incidence equals the angle of reflection as shown in Fig. 41. In the case of a sphere the angles are measured to a line (OA in Fig. 42) drawn from the center of the circle.

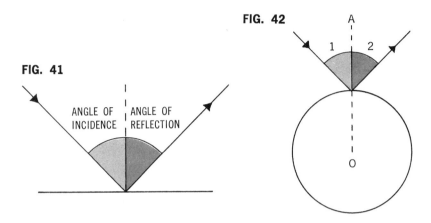

FIG. 42

FIG. 41

ANGLE OF INCIDENCE   ANGLE OF REFLECTION

The shadows in the photograph indicate that the sun was back of the cameraman. Fig. 43 shows the approximate situation. If the reflection is mirrorlike (a very smooth surface instead of rough), then most of the light from rays near A will bounce up in direction D, and not reach the cameraman (located somewhere near G). Rays near C will bounce down toward F. Rays near B will bounce toward the cameraman. Thus the straight pieces reflect much more sunlight to the camera from a position near H than from I or J.

Since the brightest lines are as light in color as the cloth adjacent to them, we may infer that the surface of the straight pieces is about as smooth and glossy as the cloth of the sphere.

How would a smooth, tube-shaped section reflect light? Fig. 43 serves to represent this situation. Some of the rays would bounce downward, as at CJF. Others would bounce

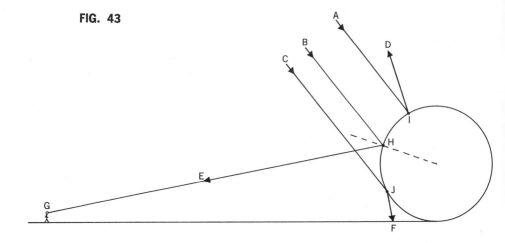

FIG. 43

upward, as at AID. Still others would bounce toward the observer, like the one at BHG. An observer viewing such a round-shaped object as this will almost always receive some reflected light from a small part of the circular section, provided the straight part of the tube is positioned across his line of vision.

Many of the straight pieces on the spherical radome are broadside to our line of vision. These are on the vertical center line of the sphere. We should get some reflected light from all such centrally located tubes—if they are tubes. Moreover the amount of light reflected from each should be about the same as from the others because of the circular nature of the shape. Thus such tube-shaped pieces should appear equally bright whether they are high or low on the sphere.

We do not observe such an equal appearance of the straight pieces. We also note bright reflections only from one small portion of the sphere. Therefore we can conclude that the pieces are not tube-shaped.

Flat-shaped pieces would give the observed distribution

of reflections since only some of them would be in the proper position to reflect light at an equal angle to the eye. But such pieces would have to be smooth and somewhat mirrorlike, otherwise we would not obtain very bright reflections from some and not from others.

So we can reasonably infer that the straight pieces on the outside of the sphere are most likely flat strips of some kind with a somewhat smooth, reflecting surface.

5. The whitest surface in the photograph is the sign. Next are the few straight lengths of the framework and the surface of the sphere at the proper position to reflect sunlight. The whitest part of the general surface of the radome is not as white as the sign. Because of the roundness of the sphere there must be some point that is just right to reflect light perfectly to the camera. The low, vertical sign is probably not at such an angle. Thus it would seem that the material of the sphere reflects substantially less light than the sign, and we might conclude that it is not a "perfect" white. We might call it a grayish white. Of course it could also be a light tint of a color, such as a light blue. But it is lower on the scale of whiteness than the sign. As an illustration, in terms of percentages the white sign might reflect 95 percent of the light striking it, while the surface of the sphere may reflect perhaps 85 percent.

However, we must be careful to limit the certainty of our conclusions. We are judging whiteness by eye, and it is always possible that our subjective judgment in this case is affected by some kind of optical illusion.

6. A scale drawing of the sphere provides important information.

First observe that the flat structure on which the radome seems to rest appears to have corners. Yet in the photograph the roof line of the surface seems to be almost straight. Place a ruler along that line. It has a slight upward bend. We can conclude that the cameraman photographed the scene from a position slightly lower than the roof of the flat structure and also that he was close to the level of the base of the sphere.

Let us now make a scale drawing of part of the sphere (Fig. 44). Draw part of a circle with center at O and radius, OA, equal to 10 cm. The diameter of this circle is 20 cm.

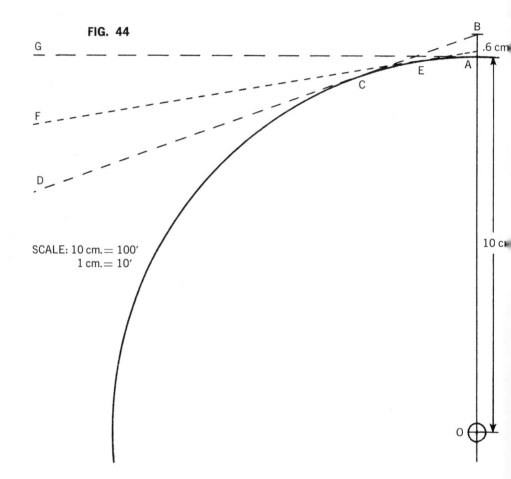

FIG. 44

SCALE: 10 cm.= 100′
      1 cm.= 10′

This corresponds to a diameter of 200 ft. Thus on your drawing 1 cm. represents 10 ft. The height of the men (AB) is about 6 ft. This distance would be represented by .6 cm. Draw this distance (AB) to represent the men on top.

Draw a line from the heads of the men (B in Fig. 44) tangent to (touching) the circle at C and extending toward D. If this line were extended to the ground, a person at that point would see only the tops of the men's heads. Obviously the camera must have been farther away than the direction toward D would indicate.

A more realistic situation would be a line of sight closer to the horizontal, something like EF. Such a line of sight would reveal most of the bodies of the men, except for a small portion of their legs. This is what we actually observe in the photograph.

Draw a horizontal line (GA) tangent to the circle at A.

Measure angle GAF with a protractor. Now use this angle to make a new drawing, reduced in scale (Fig. 45). Draw AB to represent the diameter of the sphere. Draw

FIG. 45

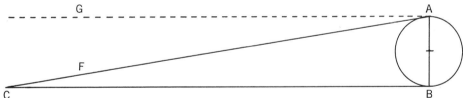

angle GAF equal to the measured angle (GAF) of the previous drawing. It crosses the ground level at C. Measure CB. It is close to 6.3 times as far from the base of the sphere as the height of the sphere. If the diameter of the sphere is 200 ft., then the camera at C is 200 ft. × 6.3, or 1,260 ft. away. This is quite a distance—about a quarter of a mile.

The margin of error is fairly large here because the

angles are small and the measurements are only approximate. A certain amount of judgment is required. But it would be reasonable to conclude from Fig. 44 that a line of sight such as BD is not likely. That line of sight gives us a ratio of 1 to 4 for height to distance, or about 800 ft. for the cameraman. Thus it would be reasonable to estimate substantially more than that. Lacking additional data, we could use the figure of 1,300 ft., keeping in mind that there might be an error of several hundred feet in this estimate.

This estimate is supported by experience with cameras. If you have taken pictures, you know that to get a person completely into a photograph he has to stand some distance away—perhaps 12 ft. The ratio of distance to height is more than 2 to 1. A similar ratio probably applies to the photograph of the sphere. Since the sphere is less than half the height of the photograph, the ratio of distance of camera to height is probably closer to 5 to 1. It would be even higher if it is an enlargement of only a portion of the negative. On this basis a rough estimate for the distance of the photographer would be at least 5 × 200 ft., or 1,000 ft. This figure provides approximate confirmation of our measurement.

7. On Puzzle Picture U the diameter of the 200-ft. sphere is measured to be 10.3 cm. The length of the boom is measured to be 16.0 cm. The actual length of the boom is therefore about $\dfrac{16.0 \text{ cm.}}{10.3 \text{ cm.}} \times 200$ ft., or 310 ft. Since this is a rough approximation, we would round out the figure to 300 ft. (If there is substantial foreshortening in the photograph, this estimate would have to be altered somewhat.) Assuming that one story of a building is about 10 ft. high, the boom could reach to the height of a 30-story building.

PUZZLE PICTURE V.   RECONSTRUCTING A SCENE

This is a scene in the Jet Propulsion Laboratory of the California Institute of Technology. There is a rocket engine on the table at the left. On the table in the right foreground we see a stand for such a rocket engine. On the back wall there are several doors and posts. What questions can you formulate about this picture? Since in this chapter we are most interested in measurement and calculation, try to formulate several questions of this nature.

RECONSTRUCTING A SCENE

The questions we shall ask about Puzzle Picture V illustrate quite fully the way in which scientific method operates. We propose to use observations, coupled with measurement, to reconstruct the original scene and to make a scale drawing of the objects in the room. Objects not in the picture, such as the camera and the lights used in taking the photograph, will be positioned on this scale drawing with a fair degree of accuracy. It is even possible to infer the heights of camera and lights above the floor and to obtain evidence for the existence of a wall a few feet to the left of the outer edge of the picture.

This Puzzle Picture will therefore be worthy of very close study. We would suggest that after trying to make the drawings yourself you follow the text step by step with your own drawings to see how the inferences are made.

Here are the questions:

1. How many lights did the cameraman use? What were their approximate positions?

2. How tall is the rocket engine?

3. What are the dimensions of the doors against the back wall?

4. How high is each shadow on the wall?

5. How high off the floor was the camera that took this picture?

6. Locate the rocket engine table on a scale map of the scene.

7. How far from the wall and from the rocket engine was the camera?

Analysis of Puzzle Picture V

1. We observe three shadows of the rocket engine on the

wall. The shadows are sharp, so concentrated lights were used.

One shadow is at the left of the engine. Therefore there must have been a light to the right of the camera. Since the shadow is close to the engine, the light must have been close to the line of sight from the camera to the engine. One might also infer that this light was higher than the engine because the shadow is lower in the picture. Actually, as we shall see later, the shadow on the wall is above the top of the engine but appears lower because more distant objects appear smaller.

2. To calculate the dimensions of the objects in the picture we need to find some "yardsticks." The following objects in the photograph may be used for that purpose:

a. Concrete blocks (of which the wall is made) are generally 8 in. high and 16 in. wide. This fact involves practical knowledge—not to be excluded in any investigation.

b. Floor tiles are generally 6-in. or 9-in. squares. The larger size is much more common and is almost universally used for industrial buildings like the one shown.

c. The height of tables is usually about 30 in.

d. The height of a doorknob from the floor is generally about 3 ft.

You might check these facts by making actual measurements at home and in other buildings.

The first step is to see if our "yardsticks" are consistent with each other. Note that we can compare distances with a ruler directly only if the objects are at the same distance from the camera, because the objects appear smaller if farther away.

First use a drawing compass (or dividers) to compare the height of the back of the table with a line of tiles between the bottoms of the table legs. A line running toward the wall cannot be used for this purpose because its length is foreshortened by perspective. An easy way to make the comparison is to mark off the dimensions along the edge of a piece of paper.

The height of the table is seen to be about equal to the length of 3½ tiles. If the tiles are 6-in. squares, the height of the table will be 3½ × 6 in., or 21 in. On the other hand, if the tiles are 9-in. squares, the height of the table will be 3½ × 9 in., or 31.5 in. The latter is quite close to the customary 30 in. and seems far more likely than the assumption of 6-in. squares. So it is reasonable to assume (subject to further checking) that the tiles are 9-in. squares.

Now compare the concrete blocks and the height of the doorknob near the right edge of the photograph. The height of the doorknob from the floor measures (on the photograph) a bit more than the height of 5 concrete blocks. This represents a height of about 5 × 8 in., or 40 in. (+). Considering the fact that the door is a bit closer to the camera than the wall, we would expect to obtain a somewhat greater height than measurements on the photograph might indicate. The fact that doorknobs are generally about 36 in. off the floor confirms our approximation of 40 in. and reinforces the validity of our assumption of an 8-in. height for the cement blocks.

Now check the height of the blocks against their width. Measure the width of 3 blocks. Compare this with the height. The width of 3 blocks is seen to be a bit less than the height of 6 blocks. Perhaps the amount of mortar between the blocks makes a difference. But for our purposes (at least for initial measurement) we will not be far off if we assume that the blocks are twice as wide as high, with dimensions of 8 in. × 16 in. We shall ignore the effect of the mortar between blocks.

Another check on our "yardsticks" is to compare the tiles with the blocks. The meeting place of the lines of tiles and the wall is somewhat lost in shadow. Nevertheless if we project two lines of tiles (AB and CD in Fig. 46) back to the approximate meeting place with the wall (EF), we can ob-

FIG. 46

tain a direct comparison with widths of blocks. Mark off EF along the edge of a piece of paper. Move this edge so as to cover a vertical line of blocks in the same area. We observe that it equals the height of about 8⅓ blocks. This represents a distance of 8⅓ × 8 in., or about 67 in. We also note that 8 floor tiles are included between E and F. This represents 8 × 9 in., or 72 in., a distance about equal to 67 in., which we measured for the equivalent blocks.

The close matching of our different assumptions about distance strengthens all of them and increases the probability that they are correct.

Now measure the height of the table in relation to the height of the rocket engine on the table. There is a problem as to just where the tops and bottoms of the table and engine begin and end. Some compromise and judgment are necessary for such measurement, and a certain amount of error is to be expected. You will find that the engine is very close to four times as high as the table. If the table is 30 in. high, then the engine is 4 × 30 in., or 120 in., or 10 ft. The top of the engine is 12½ ft. from the floor because of the 30-in. height of the table.

3. If the knob on the door at the right is 3 ft. high, then the door frame is seen to be a bit more than twice as high, or 6 ft. (+). Accurate measurement with a ruler provides a height of about 7 ft.

Additional verification is provided by the cement blocks. The door is about 11 blocks high. This gives us an estimate of the height as 11 × 8 in., or 88 in., or 7 ft. 4 in.

The width of the doors at the right is equal to the width of 6 blocks, or 6 × 16 in., or 96 in., or 8 ft.

The doors at the left are about 4½ blocks wide (for both),

or about $\dfrac{9}{2} \times$ 16 in., or 72 in., or about 6 ft. wide.

4. Heights of the shadows are estimated in the same manner. The top of the shadow on the left is seen to be about 20 blocks from the floor, or 20 × 8 in., or 160 in., or about 13 ft. 4 in.

The shadow at the right of center is two blocks higher, or 16 in. higher, or 13 ft. 4 in. plus 16 in., or about 14 ft. 8 in. high.

The shadow at the extreme right is about 4 blocks higher than that, or 32 in. plus 14 ft. 8 in., or 17 ft. 4 in. high.

5. We can make use of perspective to determine the height of the camera. The general procedure is similar to that followed in question 6 of Puzzle Picture T. All lines on the floor are in a level plane that is also parallel to the level plane at eye level. Because of perspective all of these parallel lines, if extended, will appear to meet at a point—called the *eye point*.

Place a transparent sheet of some kind over the photograph and extend three widely separated lines of the floor tiles back to where they meet, as shown in Fig. 46. Note how these lines meet approximately at a point. This eye point (G) is at the same level as the camera lens. The height on the wall of point G is 7 blocks high, or 7 × 8 in., or 56 in., or 4 ft. 8 in. off the floor. This is also the approximate height of the camera off the floor.

What circumstances concerning the taking of the picture are reasonable to infer from a 56-in. height of the camera lens? What kind of camera may have been used? One type of camera is held at waist height with the photographer looking down at a screen to view the scene. Assuming that the 56-in. height is reasonably accurate, we may infer that the camera used to take the picture was not of the type we have just described.

6. It is wise to use graph paper to make the scale drawing.

It is highly probable that the line of the floor tiles is perpendicular to the wall. If so, the perpendicular lines of graph paper will save time in marking off right angles.

First measure the distances between doors and posts on the back wall, using the cement blocks as measuring rods. In Fig. 47 the doors have been marked off on the line of the wall (AB) at C and D and the posts at E and F. In this drawing the distance between two adjacent lines on the graph paper was made to represent one foot.

Now locate the table on this drawing. Count the number of tiles from the rear leg of the table to the door. The lines become lost in shadow near the door, but with a hand lens you can see that there are 18 tiles. This represents a distance of 18×9 in., or 162 in., or $13\frac{1}{2}$ ft.

Draw line GH from the left edge of the door and extend it forward $13\frac{1}{2}$ ft. (according to the scale of the drawing). Observe that the right rear table leg (I) is about $1\frac{1}{4}$ tiles, or about 12 in., to the left of line GH. Locate this point on the drawing.

Observe that the table legs are parallel to the tile lines. Also, note that the outer edge of the left rear table leg (J in Fig. 47) is a bit more than 3 tiles from the outer edge of the right rear leg. Three tiles would be 3×9 in., or 27 in. Locate on your diagram the two rear table legs.

The points of contact of the two front table legs are not in the picture. How can we locate their positions on the scale drawing? A clue may be obtained from the floor tiles and the perspective. Draw a line from the eye point (G in

Fig. 46) to the bottom tip of the right rear table leg (I) and continue this line toward J. Trace the vertical line of the front table leg (K) to where it meets GJ at L. Point L represents the spot where the table leg touches the floor. Now mark off continuations of the spacing of the floor tiles from I toward K. We approximate 6 tiles.

A more accurate marking could be obtained with the use of a magnifying glass. Allowance might also be made for the fact that the tiles appear to be larger if they are closer to the camera, but this effect would require deeper analysis than we need to make an approximation.

The 6 tiles represent 6×9 in., or 54 in., or 4½ ft. This estimate enables us to complete the positioning of the table legs on our scale drawing.

We observe that the top of the table extends beyond the legs a few inches on all four sides. The top of the table may then be drawn on our scale drawing at MNOP.

7. The position of the camera may be approximated in several ways. First we may obtain lines of sight of various objects in the scene. Any two objects that seem to coincide on the photograph are in a straight line with the camera lens.

Note that in the Puzzle Picture the center crossbar of the engine (H in Fig. 46) is lined up with a point a few inches to the right of the edge of the door to the left. Locate point Q on the scale drawing, an estimated 3 in. to the right of the edge of the door.

Next observe that the engine is approximately centered on the table. Locate the center of the engine at point R on the scale drawing. Draw QR and extend it. The camera is somewhere near this line.

In the photograph we note that the right edge of the

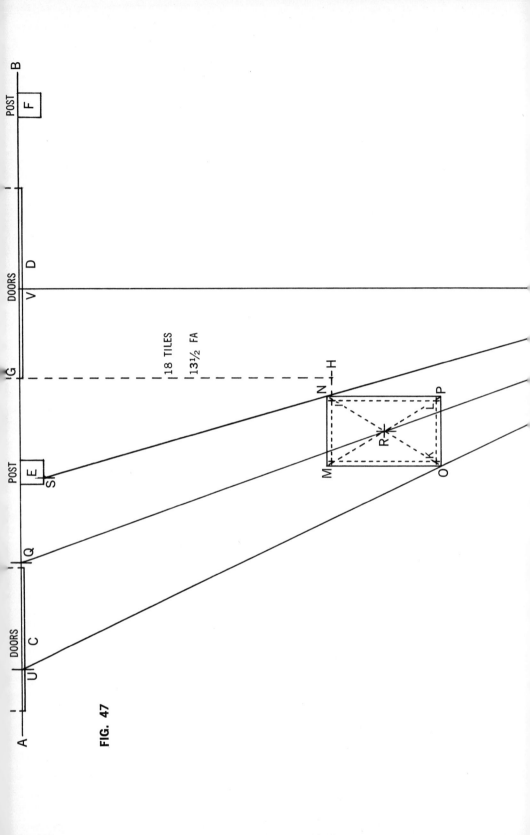

FIG. 47

SCALE: ¼" = 1 FT.

table (N) is in a line with a point (S) on the steel post against the wall. Draw SN and extend it to meet QR at T.

As a check, note that the left edge of the table lines up with a point (U) on the left door. This point is about half-way along the width of the door—or about ¼ of the width from the left edge of the door. Draw UO. It meets the other two lines at points in the region around T.

We might decide to consider the region between W and T as the approximate location of the camera. However, the very small angle at which the lines come together, the approximate estimates of the position of the table and the many other assumptions we have made indicate that we should wait a bit until an estimate is made by some other method or methods.

In the Puzzle Picture examine the two vertical posts against the wall. Note that because of perspective you see the right edge of the post at the left and the left edge of the post at the right. Very careful measurement, using a magnifying glass, indicates that we see an equal amount of the edges of both posts. Also, the posts are probably equal in size. So it seems reasonable to conclude that the camera was quite close to the midpoint between the two posts.

Locate point V, midway between the posts, and draw a perpendicular to the wall at that point. The camera is somewhere in the vicinity of that line.

Perhaps we can obtain a third guideline to reduce the uncertainty still more. We can make use of the fact that in a photograph the farther away an object is from the camera the smaller its image appears. If two objects are of equal size and one is twice as far away, it will be observed to be half as high on the photo. If it is three times as far, it is observed to be one-third the size. In other words, the observed size is inversely proportional to the distance from the camera. Or in a formula:

$$\frac{S_1}{S_2} = \frac{D_2}{D_1}$$ S is observed size
D is distance from camera

Our problem is to obtain two objects of equal size along one of our lines of sight and to measure their actual sizes. The rocket engine is one object whose size we know (approximately 10 ft. high). Back of the rocket engine is a line of blocks whose size we also know. A horizontal line of $7\frac{1}{2}$ blocks gives us a length of $7\frac{1}{2} \times 16$ in., or 120 in., or 10 ft. Measure the height of the engine on the photograph. It is about 9.8 cm. The length of $7\frac{1}{2}$ blocks on the wall back of the engine (left side of photo) is roughly 5.3 cm. Let X equal the distance of the camera from the center of the rocket engine. Measure the known distance QR on your scale drawing. It is about $16\frac{1}{4}$ ft., or approximately 16.3 ft. Then the distance of the line of blocks on the wall is X + 16.3 ft. We can now set up an equation:

$$\frac{S_1}{S_2} = \frac{D_2}{D_1}$$

In this equation:

S_1 is the measured height of the rocket on the photograph.
D_1 is the distance of the rocket from the camera.
S_2 is a measured distance on the photograph which represents 10 ft. on the back wall. (The 10-ft. distance is the same as the height of the rocket.)
D_2 is the distance from the camera of the region of the back wall used for measuring S_2.

Substituting, we obtain:

$$\frac{9.8 \text{ cm.}}{5.3 \text{ cm.}} = \frac{X + 16.3 \text{ ft.}}{X}$$

$$9.8X = 5.3X + 5.3 \times 16.3$$
$$4.5X = 86.4$$
$$X = 20 \text{ ft. (approx.)}$$

According to this calculation the camera should be 20 ft. from the center of the rocket engine at R in Fig. 47. Locate a point (X) on line QR (extended) that is 20 ft. from R.

We observe that this new approximation of the camera's position is in the general region of the previous location points and quite close to the right of the perpendicular from V.

It is now a matter of judgment as to how the three approaches are to be evaluated. Shall we just average the different locations in some way? This is a matter of individual experience, and arguments pro and con can be considered in detail.

For our purposes we shall simply average the three results by drawing a rectangle around the region that encloses X, W, T and the perpendicular line from V. All we can say at this stage is that the camera was probably located somewhere in this region.

Now that the approximate location of the camera has been determined, it would be possible to go back and reexamine some of the earlier estimates with a view to making corrections. For example, if the table were drawn a bit narrower and/or shorter, the estimates made by sighting methods would be much closer to the others. We may therefore decide to reexamine the data upon which the size and position of the table were estimated.

In scientific work this kind of correction process goes on constantly. We "zero in" on a problem by approaching it from as many directions as possible. Then we evaluate the way the estimates interlock to obtain an average value. This process involves a good deal of judgment. Then we use the average value to check back on those computations that were far off and look into them more carefully. Each approach leads to new facts which we seek to mesh still more closely with previous information. Soon we have erected an interlocking structure which is quite strong.

We shall not pursue our problem of locating the camera position any further, but you may wish to do so. We have also omitted all reference to the large structure, probably an engine base, which is observed below G in Fig. 46. You may wish to locate this object on the scale drawing and relate it to the other objects in the photograph.

The shadows on the wall also provide interesting material for further investigation. For example, in the course of the author's study of this Puzzle Picture he found it possible to estimate the probable locations of the lights used to take the picture. This was done by making scale drawings of the shadows on the wall and relating them to the rocket engine on the table. It was then possible to estimate the heights of these lights off the floor.

When the two lights on the left of the camera were placed in proper positions on the scale drawing of the drawing of the room, it turned out that they were very close to being on a line perpendicular to the back wall. This placement suggested the hypothesis that they had been suspended on a side wall. This "side wall" seemed to be several feet to the left of a perpendicular line from the edge of the door at the extreme left of the picture. In effect, we were projecting an hypothesis that there was a side wall not shown in the photograph and predicting its approximate location.

To check this hypothesis a letter was addressed to the California Institute of Technology Jet Propulsion Laboratory, where this photograph was taken, requesting confirmation of the hypothesis. The Laboratory did confirm the existence of such a wall several feet to the left of the door observed in the photograph.

Puzzle Picture V illustrates the basic features of scientific method that we have discussed in this book. You have seen how we make use of observation and experiment to gather data and to make predictions. You have observed how we employ measurement and mathematics to make our observations more precise and meaningful. You have noted the "no holds barred" approach and the attitude of the open mind that make it possible for us to probe the unknown.

Obviously the problems posed in this book cannot, by themselves, make a scientist out of you. It will require many years of application and practice at work and in everyday life to make it possible for you to become scientific in whatever you may choose to do. It is wise to start as soon as possible and to begin to apply the lessons you have learned as extensively as you can.

Format by Jean Krulis

Set in Linotype Baskerville

Composed and bound by American Book–Stratford Press

Printed by The Murray Printing Co.

HARPER & ROW, PUBLISHERS, INCORPORATED